FILMMAKERS SERIES
edited by
ANTHONY SLIDE

1. *James Whale*, by James Curtis. 1982
2. *Cinema Stylists*, by John Belton. 1983
3. *Harry Langdon*, by William Schelly. 1982
4. *William A. Wellman*, by Frank Thompson. 1983
5. *Stanley Donen*, by Joseph Casper. 1983
6. *Brian DePalma*, by Michael Bliss. 1983
7. *J. Stuart Blackton*, by Marian Blackton Trimble. 1985
8. *Martin Scorsese and Michael Cimino*, by Michael Bliss. 1985
9. *Franklin J. Schaffner*, by Erwin Kim. 1985
10. *D. W. Griffith at Biograph*, by Cooper C. Graham et al. 1985
11. *Some Day We'll Laugh: An Autobiography*, by Esther Ralston. 1985
12. *The Memoirs of Alice Guy Blach*, trans. by Roberta and Simone Blaché. 1986
13. *Leni Riefenstahl and Olympia*, by Cooper C. Graham. 1986
14. *Robert Florey*, by Brian Taves. 1987
15. *Henry King's America*, by Walter Coppedge. 1986
16. *Aldous Huxley and Film*, by Virginia M. Clark. 1987
17. *Five American Cinematographers*, by Scott Eyman. 1987
18. *Cinematographers on the Art and Craft of Cinematography*, by Anna Kate Sterling. 1987
19. *Stars of the Silents*, by Edward Wagenknecht. 1987
20. *Twentieth Century-Fox*, by Aubrey Solomon. 1988
21. *Highlights and Shadows: The Memoirs of a Hollywood Cameraman*, by Charles G. Clarke. 1989
22. *I Went That-a-Way: The Memoirs of a Western Film Director*, by Harry L. Fraser; edited by Wheeler Winston Dixon and Audrey Brown Fraser. 1990
23. *Order in the Universe: The Films of John Carpenter*, by Robert C. Cumbow. 1990
24. *The Films of Freddie Francis*, by Wheeler Winston Dixon. 1991
25. *Hollywood Be Thy Name*, by William Bakewell. 1991
26. *The Charm of Evil: The Life and Films of Terence Fisher*, by Wheeler Winston Dixon. 1991
27. *Lionheart in Hollywood: The Autobiography of Henry Wilcoxon*, with Katherine Orrison. 1991
28. *William Desmond Taylor: A Dossier*, by Bruce Long. 1991
29. *The Films of Leni Riefenstahl*, 2nd ed., by David B. Hinton. 1991

Filmmakers Series (continued)

30. *Hollywood Holyland: The Filming and Scoring of "The Greatest Story Ever Told,"* by Ken Darby. 1992
31. *The Films of Reginald LeBorg: Interviews, Essays, and Filmography,* by Wheeler Winston Dixon. 1992
32. *Memoirs of a Professional Cad,* by George Sanders, with Tony Thomas. 1992
33. *The Holocaust in French Film,* by André Pierre Colombat. 1993
34. *Robert Goldstein and "The Spirit of '76,"* edited and compiled by Anthony Slide. 1993
35. *Those Were the Days, My Friend: My Life in Hollywood with David O. Selznick and Others,* by Paul Macnamara. 1993
36. *The Creative Producer,* by David Lewis; edited by James Curtis. 1993
37. *Reinventing Reality: The Art and Life of Rouben Mamoulian,* by Mark Spergel. 1993
38. *Malcolm St. Clair: His Films, 1915-1948,* by Ruth Anne Dwyer. 1995
39. *Beyond Hollywood's Grasp: American Filmmakers Abroad, 1914-1945,* by Harry Waldman. 1994
40. *A Steady Digression to a Fixed Point,* by Rose Hobart. 1994
41. *Radical Juxtaposition: The Films of Yvonne Rainer,* by Shelley Green. 1994
42. *Company of Heroes: My Life as an Actor in the John Ford Stock Company,* by Harry Carey, Jr. 1994
43. *Strangers in Hollywood: A History of Scandinavian Actors in American Films from 1910 to World War II,* by Hans J. Wollstein. 1994
44. *Charlie Chaplin: Intimate Close-Ups,* by Georgia Hale, edited with an introduction and notes by Heather Kiernan. 1995
45. *The Word Made Flesh: Catholicism and Conflict in the Films of Martin Scorsese,* by Michael Bliss. 1995
46. *W. S. Van Dyke's Journal: White Shadows in the South Seas (1927-1928) and other Van Dyke on Van Dyke,* edited and annotated by Rudy Behlmer. 1996
47. *Music from the House of Hammer: Music in the HammerHorror Films 1950-1980,* by Randall D. Larson. 1996
48. *Directing: Learn from the Masters,* by Tay Garnett. 1996
49. *Featured Player: An Oral Autobiography of Mae Clarke,* edited with an introduction by James Curtis. 1996
50. *A Great Lady: A Life of the Screenwriter Sonya Levien,* by Larry Ceplair. 1996

SONYA LEVIEN, ca. 1932

Fox Film Corporation publicity still taken at the time she received a nomination for the Academy Award for Best Adaptation for *State Fair*. (*Courtesy of the Academy of Motion Picture Arts and Sciences and Twentieth Century-Fox.*)

A Great Lady

A Life of the Screenwriter Sonya Levien

Larry Ceplair

Filmmakers, No. 50

The Scarecrow Press, Inc.
Lanham, Md., & London

SCARECROW PRESS, INC.

Published in the United States of America
by Scarecrow Press, Inc.
4720 Boston Way
Lanham, Maryland 20706

4 Pleydell Gardens, Folkestone
Kent CT20 2DN, England

Copyright © 1996 by Larry Ceplair

All rights reserved. No part of this publication may be reproduced, stored in a retrieval system, or transmitted in any form or by any means, electronic, mechanical, photocopying, recording, or otherwise, without the prior permission of the publisher.

British Cataloguing-in-Publication Information Available

Library of Congress Cataloging-in-Publication Data

Ceplair, Larry.
A great lady : a life of the screenwriter Sonya Levien / Larry Ceplair.
p.   cm.—(Filmmakers ; no. 50)
Includes bibliographical references and index.
1. Levien, Sonya, 1898–1960—Biography. 2. Women screenwriters—United States—Biography. I. Title II. Series: Filmmakers series ; no. 50.
PS3523.E7987Z63   1996   808.2'309—dc20   [B]   95-43945

ISBN 0-8108-3092-2 (cloth: alk.paper)

⊖™ The paper used in this publication meets the minimum requirements of American National Standard for Information Sciences—Permanence of Paper for Printed Library Materials, ANSI Z39.48–1984. Manufactured in the United States of America.

For the largeness of their love,
I gratefully dedicate this book
to my mother, Betty Ceplair,
and to Andy, Athena, Ken, and Sheila.

Contents

Preface *vii*

Chapter 1
Family Background 1

Chapter 2
At *The Metropolitan* 19

Chapter 3
The Movie Industry and the Scenario Writer 33

Chapter 4
Early Scenario Career 53

Chapter 5
At Fox and Twentieth Century-Fox 71

Chapter 6
At M-G-M 103

Endnotes *121*

Filmography *137*

Index *155*

About the Author *161*

Preface

Ever since Steven Englund and I completed our history of the blacklist era in Hollywood, which centered on the political activities of screenwriters, I have wanted to write a book on them and their screen work. We had discovered, in the course of our research, that an amazing number of fictions surrounded the life and work of Hollywood studio writers. I wanted to provide an objective account, but I did not know how to proceed. A prosopography made no sense: Too many screenwriters worked in too many different epochs at too many different studios. An analysis of the screenwriting process, focusing on a few selected writers and scripts, promised to bore both author and reader.[1]

A biography, as a lens through which to view the process and the craft, suggested itself. That required a successful screenwriter, one who had enjoyed a long career spanning several industrial epochs, and a cache of personal material. Finally, I had one additional desideratum: I wanted my subject to be a woman. Female screenwriters, I thought, had not received their due.[2]

Sonya Levien's life and career not only met my basic requirements, they also provided a perspective on the choices success-oriented women with families believed they had to make during the early decades of the twentieth century. Having come of age in the Progressive era, Levien symbolized the "new woman": independent, career-oriented, and politically radical. But her family background and Russian-Jewish culture had implanted strong maternal drives in her. As a result, though she seemed to be moving inexorably upward in her chosen fields—magazine editing and writing and movie writing—Levien regularly had to measure the effect of professional choice on her family.

In addition, in the process of becoming one of the movie industry's highest-paid and most-credited writers, she shucked all vestiges of her political radicalism. She maintained a very low political posture in Hollywood, and her screen characters bore no resemblance to the type of women she had known or the type of woman she had been. The Hollywood studio system offered little room in its genres for the political and gender consciousness she had once exemplified, and Levien was either not clever enough to figure out how to infiltrate Levien-type women into her scripts or too insecure to try, so her plots and characters rarely transcended the melodramatic format.

Levien possessed a certain plot cleverness or dexterity and an editor's willingness to cut and paste. She succeeded as a screenwriter because she knew how to adapt stories, plays, and novels into "entertaining," filmable movie scripts, wrote quickly, and made, without argument, whatever script changes her supervisors directed. In addition, she willingly doctored other writers' problem scripts, never missed a deadline, and worked as many hours as necessary to solve script problems. Seemingly without ego investment in the words she wrote, she rarely complained, and she helped anyone who asked. Every person who worked with her adored her. All I have spoken with called her "a great lady."[3]

Along the way, I encountered a few obstacles. Her daughter, Tamara Hovey Gold, chose not to provide me with any material or information not available in the papers she contributed to the Huntington Library, and those papers, especially those from 1945-60, seem to have been carefully pruned. Surviving family members (mainly nephews and nieces in New York) have only snippets of memories and no papers. I am especially grateful to Robert Levien, Sonya's nephew, for his efforts to ransack his memory and his papers for useful information.

Facing major gaps in the Russian and Lower East Side stories, I have drawn generalized milieus or tableaus based on the memories of others, with the tentative suggestion that these depictions shed some light on the influences that surrounded the Leviens in both places. I have also made careful use of some of the material in Ms. Gold's autobiographical novel, *Among the Survivors*, for material on Ms. Levien's married life with Carl Hovey.

Production records or script material for all her screen work was not readily available. The Turner Entertainment Co. does not allow access to the legal files of M-G-M and RKO; Sony Pictures did not respond to my request for access to Columbia material; Samuel Goldwyn, Jr., did not allow me access to the material on *The Cowboy and the Lady* on deposit at the Margaret Herrick Library of the Academy of Motion Picture Arts and Sciences; and very little remains from the work she did during the 1920s.

On the other hand, Ned Comstock, overseer of the Cinema/Television Library at the University of Southern California, helped me immensely with the Fox and M-G-M materials under his aegis, and Stuart Ng, overseer of the Warner Bros. material at USC, did likewise. At the Herrick Library, Howard Prouty and Samuel Gill assisted me with the Paramount, Pathé, and Goldwyn efforts. Rose Hatch and Lorayne Jurist greatly eased my path to use of the Twentieth Century-Fox legal records at UCLA, and Paul Camp and Brigitte Kueppers of the UCLA Arts Library-Special Collections provided them for me. Sue Hodson provided much-needed assistance with the Levien papers at the Huntington Library. I am also grateful to Gretchen Feltes (NYU Law School), Erika Gorder and Nancy Cricco (NYU University Archives), Bernard R. Crystal (Rare Books and Manuscripts Library, Columbia University), and Wendy Thomas (Schlesinger Library, Radcliffe College). Finally, I thank those scholars who responded to my letter queries: Kevin Brownlow, Lawrence C. Kelly, Pat McGilligan, and Kenneth Philp.

In May 1992, and again in August 1993, I requested Freedom of Information-Privacy Act material from the Federal Bureau of Investigation. I was informed, on August 28, 1995, that it was presently processing requests made in April 1992.

For permission to reprint archival material, I wish to thank The Huntington Library; Rare Book and Manuscript Library, Columbia University; Special Collections, UCLA Research Library; Tamiment Collection, Bobst Library, NYU; Yale University Library; Paramount Pictures; Samuel Goldwyn Co.; Twentieth Century-Fox (with special thanks to Rebecca Herrera); Warner Bros.; and Turner Entertainment Co.

Chapter 1

Family Background

Sonya Levien's story begins in the Pale of Settlement, that area carved from Poland, Lithuania, and Russia as a restrictive area for the Jewish people entrapped in and oppressed by the Russian Empire. There, in Panimunik, a little village of less than fifty homes forty miles west of Dvinsk (present-day Daugavpils, Latvia), Julius (b. ca. 1863) and Fanny (b. ca. 1865) Opesken conceived their first child, Sara, who was born on December 25, 1888.[1] (Sonya, the Russian diminutive of Sara, would later alter her birthdate to 1898.)

The Jewish population of the cities of this area had grown rapidly since May 1882, when the Interior Ministry's Central Committee on Jewish Affairs imposed Temporary Rules as part of Czar Alexander III's (1881-94) response to the assassination of his father, Alexander II (1855-81). Capping a year of officially sanctioned violence against the Jews of the Pale, the Temporary Rules prohibited new Jewish settlements in the countryside of the Pale and Jewish business activity on Sundays or Christian holidays. Local authorities responded by expelling Jews from the villages.

Many of the expelled emigrated to the United States (the numbers increased sharply from 8,193 in 1881 to 31,889 in 1889), a much smaller stream trickled toward Palestine, and others moved into the cities of the Pale. The number of Jewish people in Vilna climbed from 37,909 in 1875 to 63,841 in 1897 (or 41 percent of the population), while Dvinsk's rose to

32,400 (44 percent). Though a government circular eventually condemned further pogroms, it also imposed a series of disabling rules and regulations on the urban Jews, dislodging them from liberal professions, blocking their access to secondary and higher education, and more strictly enforcing military obligations. (In the early 1890s, the Jews, though only 12.3 percent of the population of Vilna, provided 17.2 percent of army recruits.)

In both village and city, the vast majority of the Jews were impoverished workers or artisans. Life in the villages, however, was less crowded. Abraham Cahan remembers the contrast between Podberezy, the small village in which he was born in 1860, and Vilna, the city to which the family moved when he was six:

> Podberezy was a small town. Turn any corner and there was a garden with flowers and the free air and the wide heavens. Her breath was fresh. But Vilna was only streets and more streets. Her houses seemed to me dark and forbidding, her earth buried under cobblestones. There was no plumbing. The stench in the courtyards seemed to issue from the bricks of the buildings. No wind seemed strong enough to carry it off.

In Podberezy, the Cahans lived in a one-story wooden building that housed four families in separate apartments leading from an entrance hallway, whereas in Vilna they lived in an apartment adjoining a tavern in a partially covered courtyard. His father, in their village years, had been a *melamed,* a *cheder* teacher, and his mother taught girls how to read and write. In Vilna, they tended a tavern.[2]

Handwork or the keeping of very small shops occupied most Jewish males. They dominated the hosiery, leather, boot, tobacco, and paper trades. They were, remembers Avraham Kariv, "plain working people, engaged in the many trades and crafts that provided the necessities of daily life for the non-Jewish population of town and countryside." He called them a "tribe of the poor," who "led lives of purity and moderation," speaking Yiddish almost exclusively.[3] It is estimated that Jews comprised 77 percent of the tradesman population and that 99 percent used Yiddish as their everyday language.

Though they were situated in the poorest portion of the Pale of Settlement, Vilna's Jews were an intellectually and socially creative community, and Vilna became known as the Jerusalem of Lithuania. The *Haskalah,* or Jewish enlightenment, took a strong hold there, leading its followers away from assimilation and toward an exaltation of Hebrew. Much less affected by the emotional appeal of *Chasidism* than the rest of the Pale, the Jews of Lithuania favored the *musar* movement, with its focus on the ethical themes and moral attributes found in the *Talmud* and *Midrash.* Vilna was also the site of one of the first chapters of *Hovevei Zion* and the earliest Jewish artisan guilds (*hevrah ba'alay melakhah*) and the birthplace of Russian Jewish socialism.

Jewish political radicalism built slowly. Although some joined with the Russian *narodnikii* (populists), most notably Marc Natanson, who organized the Chaikovsky circles in St. Petersburg, Jews as a whole remained aloof, and Jewish *narodnikii* scorned the Jewish masses. Lev Deutsch remarked: "For us there were essentially no Jewish workers. ...The Jews had to dissolve among the native population."[4] But increasing numbers of young Jewish students became socially conscious, and Vilna served as a point of contact between Russian and western European radicals and a transit point for literature, escapees, and prisoners.

At the Vilna Rabbinical Seminary, Aaron Zundelevich organized a clandestine student circle, a network to smuggle prohibited literature and fugitives, a chapter of Land and Freedom, and the first successful clandestine printing press. A member of that circle, Aaron Lieberman, devoted some of his work to winning the Jewish masses to socialism. At the same time, Vilna tobacco workers organized one of the first documented strikes of Jewish workers. But emigration to avoid arrest stripped the movement of some of its best leaders, and an ideological struggle commenced between the *narodnikii* and the Marxists. Many of the intelligentsia of the study circles refused to engage in mass agitation, and those who did pay attention to the Jewish masses concentrated on teaching them to read and speak Russian. Indeed, the "typical 'enlightened' Jewish worker...went about dressed in a Russian black shirt, carrying a Russian book under his arm and with Russian on his lips. ...[Yashka, from Dvinsk] affected a knowledge of Russian which was far from perfect. [He] spoke a mixture of Russian and Yiddish that 'was a sign of education, or enlightenment.'"[5]

Russian authorities, meanwhile, maintained a close watch over all Russians and Jews advocating changes in the polity or society. Periodically, those deemed particularly dangerous were arrested and consigned by administrative decree to Siberia, including, in 1889 or 1890, Julius Opesken. Sonya said her father had a remote connection with a radical newspaper, but very few radical newspapers existed in Russia during the 1880s, and none in the Pale. It is possible that he was a printer, preparer, or distributor of agitational pamphlets or part of a network that smuggled in material printed abroad by exiles. Printers were well represented in the study circles and were considered the intellectuals of workers.

Sonya also said her father adhered to the anarchist ideas of Prince Peter Kropotkin, but she did not indicate when. Kropotkin had been imprisoned by Russian authorities in 1874, before he had written anything that might have reached the Pale and, during the twenty years following his 1876 escape from prison, he maintained only scanty contacts with Russia and a limited interest in the Russian radical movement. However, since many of the articles Kropotkin wrote during the 1880s were reprinted as pamphlets in virtually every European language, including Yiddish, it is possible some may have trickled into the Pale.[6]

Opesken probably joined a *narodnik* study circle. Abraham Cahan, who at age twenty began reading the clandestine literature of Land and Freedom and People's Will, the two main *narodnik* organizations, became involved with a circle of Vilna "nihilists" and recollected his feelings: "Life took on new meaning. Our society was built on injustices that could be erased. All could be equal. All could be brothers!...It could be done! It must be done! All must be ready to sacrifice even life itself for this new kind of world." The members gathered a small number of Jewish workers into their cellar quarters to teach them Russian grammar and the principles of socialism. "We regarded ourselves as human beings, not as Jews. There was only one remedy for the world's ills and that was socialism."[7]

But Opesken was arrested and exiled before a distinct Jewish socialism focusing on organizing the Jewish working class emerged. While he worked in the mines in Siberia, Sonya, her mother, and two brothers lived with Julius's father, a rabbi and *meladem*. Sonya remembered

> the winters, how bitter, how cold, and the laughter and sadness of our people; and the tall dark woods all around our village. I did not dare go in them for fear of the wolves; their shining yellow eyes peered out from among the trees. Through the long hard winters we were bundled up like sacks tied in the middle, but on holidays there were festivals, singing, deep drinking, and bright embroidered costumes.[8]

Adeline Schulberg, wife of producer Ben Schulberg and mother of screenwriter Budd Schulberg, was also born in that village. Though she left when she was one or two years old, she was later told tales of a "Fiddler-on-the Roof"-type village, oppressed by constant antisemitism and recurring pogroms.[9]

Grandfather Opesken was a very learned man. He and his "closest friend," the priest of the Greek Catholic Church, "were not only the village teachers, but adjudicators when the villagers quarreled and lay doctors when they fell ill."[10] He was also an intensely religious man, insisting that Sonya "had to tender the Lord my piety in behalf of my father, who, I was constantly reminded, was no doubt forbidden to say his prayers as often as a good Jew must." Thus, in an unusual move for that time and place, Sonya's grandfather provided her with a course of instruction comparable to that a Jewish male would receive. While parents spared no effort to send their sons to *cheders* and then *yeshivot* to learn Jewish law—"the ether which permeated the entire universe of Lithuanian Jewry"[11] —Jewish girls rarely received a formal education. They were only expected to know how to conduct the domestic rituals and maintain the home.

Grandfather Opesken, however, had six-year-old Sonya reading from the *Talmud* for two hours each morning before breakfast, and later the *Shulhan'Aruk*—"voluminous books containing precise standards of practice." As a result, "The thought of wrongdoing petrified me and the relation of disobedience and punishment was ever before my mind's eye....If I had any impulse to disobey, the penalty immediately visualized itself and I could not get free of it."[12] He also taught her to speak Russian, Hebrew, German, and some French and Latin.

In 1891, her father, aided by a German engineer, escaped from exile and emigrated to the United States. Fearing extradition, he assumed his rescuer's name—Levien. For five years, he worked, probably as a peddler of notions, to earn the money to bring over his wife and children. Finally, in 1896, they arrived, moving into a cold-water flat on the Lower East Side of Manhattan, part of the flood of 150,000 Russian Jews who came to New York City between 1891 and 1900. Two more sons (Nathan and Edward) were born in this country, and Sonya, Arnold, Max, and their parents received their naturalization papers, in the name of Levien, in 1905.[13]

Though the adult Sonya retained both her Russian accent and a positive image of the Russian people, admiring "their wonderful simplicity," idealism, and sincerity,[14] she exhibited no special attachment to its culture or, after 1917, its politics.

Her father joined the thinning ranks of Jewish anarchists who, at the time of his arrival, were shifting from a revolutionary utopianism to a more pragmatic style of work in labor unions, branches of the Workmen's Circle, and literary clubs and libraries. Peter Kropotkin was by far the most popular writer among Jewish anarchists in the United States. The first anarchist thinker to formulate a scientific basis for his anarchist principles and the revolutionary who most strongly insisted on a moral base for the revolution and ensuing libertarian society, Kropotkin appealed to both the rationalist and ethical sensibilities of the Russian Jewish emigré. All the Yiddish anarchist periodicals reprinted his articles and excerpts from his books, and his 1897 and 1901 visits to the United States gave a tremendous lift to the Jewish anarchist movement.[15]

In a comment on a book or story about radicalism and Russian Jewish immigrants to the United States, written when she was a fiction reader, Levien describes a person who might well have been her father. Russian Jews in America, she explained, did not adhere to anarcho-syndicalist groups like the Industrial Workers of the World because that involved "the risking of one's personal life, family, livelihood, and bodily comfort. The very young Jew, 18 or 19, might go into it for a year or so, but not the middle-aged Jew. He usually becomes a conservative at that age; if not, then he is a philosophical radical."

> Now take Helena's father [the fictional character in the story]. If he were a Russian Jew, born and brought up there, he might very well have been a Nihilist, but then, he would not have been educated by his parents except in rabbinical law. He would have gone to the gymnasia, neglected his studies but would have picked up a tremendous lot of information from books and student life, fought with his parents,

thrown himself into the Russian revolution. He would stay in the Revolutionary movement for three to five years and in that time would go to the limit and be killed or quit, perhaps marry and become an ineffectual conservative....He might have emigrated to America and gone on leading this half-awake sort of life. BUT NEVER AGAIN WOULD HE HAVE TAKEN ACTIVE PART IN A RADICAL REVOLUTIONARY MOVEMENT. It would all be too tame after what he had gone through.

Even if he remained a radical, she continued, he would keep his radicalism separate from his family.

[H]e is usually a very poor, hardworking laborer and conscienciously [sic] belongs to the union, is *logical and constructive* in his view on the Labor Movement, and against the I.W.W. movement as too wild....The Jew, whether Russian or otherwise, is above else, a reasoning being. He is logical, he is constructive, but he is not wastefully heroic.

She would later note that her father was "bitterly anti-Bolshevik, his radicalism is of another kind."[16]

Looking back on her own political attitudes, Levien wrote, in 1918: "When I first came to this country and lived on the East Side, I naturally joined a group of agitators—socialists, anarchists, and single-taxers—but the majority were socialists. We signed ourselves, 'Yours for the Revolution.'" Though she read "innumerable red pamphlets bound up in paraffin paper," her "staunch belief in socialism was not due to the pamphlets I read or my association with the Group. Poverty had embittered young life for me. I had come here to the trumpet call of liberty. A feather-duster factory swallowed up my teens at four dollars a week."[17]

All the Levien children worked their way through high school and college and contributed money to their parents. Sonya alone manifested a radical consciousness and activism; her brothers became engineers of various types. "In my day," she later noted, "I've been a whole-hearted anarchist, a socialist and a suffragist, and I remember once making a most eloquent speech about the higher idealism of free love."[18]

Sonya attended a public grammar school, the main institutional agency for the cultural transformation of the European immigrant to the United States. Since public education was universally acknowledged as the vehicle of Americanization for most young foreign-born children, foreign-born parents willingly sent their boys and girls to learn how to be different from them. In addition, assimilated Jews had established a Hebrew Free School Society (1864), which merged with two other educational institutions to become the Educational Alliance (1892). Its function was to Americanize older immigrants and dissolve the Jewish ghetto through programs of English language instruction, vocational training, lectures, art lessons, and libraries. The directors of the Alliance cooperated closely with the Board of Education, at one point urging the board to expand its vocational education offerings for girls aged 12-14, who could not afford to attend high school.[19]

Sonya completed grammar school, but the family's finances could not support her through high school. Very few immigrant children attended high school in the first decade of the twentieth century. The first public high school in Manhattan opened in 1897, and there were none in the lower portion of the island. According to the *Forward,* the choices for a female grammar school graduate were few:

> When a grown girl emigrates to America, she becomes either a finisher or an operator. Girls who have grown up here do not work at these "greenhorn" trades. They become either salesladies or typists. A typist represents a compromise between a teacher and a finisher.
>
> Salaries for typists are very low....But typists have more *yikhes* [status] than shopgirls; it helps them get a husband; they come in contact with a more refined class of people.[20]

At the end of her elementary school education in 1901 or

1902, Sonya decided to emancipate herself from factory work and become a secretary. She secured a loan of $36 from a member of the school board to pay for a course in stenography. (It took her four years to repay it.) She worked for four years for "a well-known man," became involved in settlement work and labor union activity, and continued her education at the Educational Alliance, where, in the summer of 1903, she met Rose Pastor.

Pastor, born in Poland in 1879, had emigrated to London, then to Cleveland, where she worked for twelve years in cigar factories. She briefly adhered to the Socialist Party of America and unsuccessfully attempted to organize cigar workers. In 1901, she became interested in poetry and writing and began to contribute material to the *Jewish Daily News* in New York City. She moved there in 1903. In her unpublished autobiography, she wrote:

> At the Jewish Educational Alliance two groups of girls met. One from a club at the University Settlement; the other from a club at the Alliance. They formed one club and sent a request to me to come and be their leader for the summer months... We met once a week in a room of the Alliance Building... where we talked, read books and papers, and discussed individual and home problems. At times, I spoke to them about Socialism and passed on the few vague concepts which were then mine on the subject. These talks stirred and interested the girls, and I was glad. But soon, the meeting place in the Alliance was denied us, for some reason; so we gathered in the little three-room flat on lower Grand Street to which my mother and several of the children had come. There, on chairs and boxes and window-ledges, on tables and floors and beds, we'd sit and hold earnest confab. At the summer's end, their club leaders returned, and since the understanding had been that I would stay only until the return of their leaders, I refused to be an "interloper," and promptly left the girls to the old leadership. But they refused to accept the change. They would waylay me as I came from the office, and hammer away at my resistance. Sonia [sic] Levien—one of the girls—

Sonia of the blue eyes and black hair, and the smile as kind as my grandfather's, cried real tears as we stood at the curb debating the matter. Finally, I relented, and offered a compromise. I would visit the [University Settlement] Club, provided the leader raised no objections.[21]

At the University Settlement, Pastor met James G. P. Stokes. They married in 1905, with Sonya in attendance, and, following their honeymoon, Sonya became Mrs. Stokes's secretary.[22] In 1906, Mrs. Stokes, disenchanted with settlement work, began to attend Socialist Party and Women's Trade Union League meetings. The effect on Sonya can only be guessed. She recalled, "Mr. Stokes was away a great deal and I took advantage of his wonderful library to prepare for my regents examinations." She also worked at the University Settlement, perhaps helping to edit the *University Settlement Studies,* which appeared from 1905-08, with investigative reports on various aspects of life and conditions on the Lower East Side. Aspiring to be a writer, she began contributing humorous squibs to *Life* as a means of earning college tuition fees and contributing to the support of her parents.

In September 1906, having received a Regents Qualifying Certificate for Law Students, Levien enrolled at New York University Law School as a candidate for a Certificate of Law. Toward the end of her life, she told an interviewer, "I studied law because I never thought I would make a living writing. I was always scared that I might starve."[23]

Sonya continued sending material to *Life* in the form of the comical sayings of an alcoholic Irish teacher at the law school and essays on woman's suffrage. She also wrote skits for university productions. One of the students wrote about her:

> There's a maid at N.Y.U.
> Who of friends has quite a few,
> Not only at the law school but at other places too;
> For her time is also spent

> At an east-side settlement,
> Where she trains the "Wisdom Seekers" in the proper
>   things to do.
>
> And when not long ago,
> There was held the yearly show,
> It was really very pleasant for the people to behold,
> How the children one and all,
> Did her bidding but at call,
> And presented her with flowers that far more than words
>   foretold—
>
> How they loved her for her style,
> For her sunny patient smile,
> For her tender earnest manner and her personality;
> In their eyes there's but one queen—
> That's the teacher, Miss Levien,
> And a better queen or subjects have historians yet to
>   see.[24]

In 1907, she secured a job as secretary to Samuel Merwin, editor of *Success*. He designed a course of study in English literature for her and then began to assign her various editorial and writing tasks. Four years later, with *Success* nearing its end, Levien applied for a job at *Collier's* in a letter describing the breadth of her magazine experience:

> I have done practically every possible thing that there is to be done in the getting out of a big magazine. There was my department "Concerning Women," which consisted of editorial comment on current events; then I had charge of the women's page ["Women Everywhere"] which dealt chiefly with the town problems of interest to women, home talks, household hints and social functions. My long articles, mostly on women interests, have in every case met with appreciative responses.
>   As for office routine work—for the past three years I have

done all of the ma[n]uscript reading. My province also included the rewriting [of] articles and stories, and where the idea was found worth while, I have collaborated with the author.

I have edited manuscripts, worked on titles and subtitles, and have done final proof-reading, and at time took charge of the make-up end.

My law training has made it possible for me to handle investigations, or gather suggestions and materials for articles; as you know, I have taken active part in all of the editorial planning.

At the end of the letter, she noted that it had "been difficult to write this bit of self-advertising."

In an unsent draft, perhaps partly written for comic relief but clearly also to express her dissatisfaction with women's opportunities in magazine publishing, she wrote:

I am peddling my wares and so if *Collier's* is in need of a first class A.1. woman editor who can do anything from appearing overexcited to interesting work, pp. writing or mss. reading—why just tell them that you know of one, won't you please.

Somehow I don't believe that *Collier's* has much toleration for women sub-editors, and I don't blame them, but if they are willing to consider one, I should love to get the opportunity to prove myself.[25]

Years later, she commented on the changes that had occurred in the professional world's perspective of a professional woman:

That time [1912] was an era of feminine ministers in the world, the first women with missions outside of their homes. Nowadays [1925] women have given up missions and go upon the basis of each working for herself. The novelty of their being in business is over. They must compete with men on equal terms. It's a struggle between men and women in nearly every profession. When I first started, men didn't fear us because we were a novelty and they treated us with amusement and courtesy, but now we are a thorn in the field of competition, another factor to fight. The relationship is entirely different than when I was a youngster.[26]

During this time, Sonya became friends with Frances Perkins and a lover of Sinclair Lewis. Perkins had come to New York City in 1909 on a Russell Sage Foundation fellowship to compile a survey of Hell's Kitchen. In 1910, she earned an M.A. in economics and sociology at Columbia University, published her first article, "Some Notes Concerning Undernourished Children," in *The Survey*, and became secretary of the New York Consumers' League.

Lewis had not yet published the novels that would bring him fame; he was one of a number of aspiring writers in Greenwich Village. Many years later, Sonya told Philip Alan Friedman, a researcher:

> I saw a lot of Sinclair Lewis when he was working as a publicist for a publishing house.... At that time I was Assistant Editor on a magazine called *Success* and later another short-lived magazine called *The National Post*. It must have been around 1910 or 1911. ...As the saying goes, "we kept company" for several years. ...Yes, we talked of marriage—seriously.

She provided a similar account to biographer Mark Schorer, who wrote that Levien frequently protested about Lewis's drinking, while he accused her of being conventional.[27]

Sara A. Levien applied for admission to the New York Bar in September 1909, giving as her address, 456 E. 141st St., the Bronx. But she quickly discovered "that I would not make a good lawyer after all. I was too sympathetic, my emotions too near the surface to take the clever advantages that a successful lawyer must." She told one of her future colleagues, William Ludwig, that her first encounter with the court calendar call finished her. "'I'm ready,' she told the judge. 'Are you now, darling,' he replied. Blushing a fiery red, Sonya ran from the court room and never returned."[28] She continued to work at *Success,* where she was promoted to fiction reader.

Success ceased publication in December 1911 and, a few months later, Levien met with Alice Stone Blackwell, editor of *The Woman's Journal,* the main organ of the woman suffrage movement. A series of disagreements between Blackwell and the board of the National American Woman Suffrage Association had blossomed over the location and look of the journal and its financial problems. In a letter to the state presidents, Blackwell wrote: "At a special meeting of the official Board in April, Miss Sara A. Levein [sic] was engaged as assistant editor." The board also named her as business manager, even though the contract of the incumbent, Agnes E. Ryan, did not expire until June 30. According to Blackwell, Ryan agreed to divide the work with Sonya. "Miss Levein comes to us highly recommended, and I hope that she and Miss Ryan together will make a strong team."

Levien's name first appeared on the masthead of the July 6 issue, as "Managing Editor." A few articles, mainly concerned with increasing the newspaper's circulation, appeared under her byline. On October 5, Levien's name ceased to appear, replaced by that of Agnes Ryan, the former business manager. A short announcement stated, "The national treasury being hard pressed, Miss Blackwell has undertaken to be responsible for the expense of publishing *The Woman's Journal,* and has also taken over the business management, which will now be in the hands of Miss Agnes E. Ryan."[29]

Either Levien and Ryan did not make a strong team, or Blackwell and Levien did not get along, or Levien simply decided she could not make a sufficient impact on the newspaper. An undated set of notes indicates that she wanted to make major changes in the news-gathering operation by adding a news service, reporters, makeup editor, and artists. *The Journal,* she noted, was too dependent on information derived from personal letters sent by the various state organizations. She also noted, and perhaps that became the obstacle she could not overcome, that no money was available to transform the journal into a modern newspaper.

Though she later claimed she spent a year in Boston editing *The Woman's Journal,* it is probable that she was back in New York before the end of 1912, searching for a new job. She secured a position on *The Metropolitan,* hired by its new co-editor, Carl Hovey (1875-1956). According to Hovey, they first communicated when she sent a short story to *The Metropolitan.* "There was something about it I liked," he later told S. N. Behrman, "but I thought it was too long. I sent a note to Sonya asking her to cut it and send it in again. She wrote back—rather peppery—to say that *Ainslee's* had accepted the story—length and all."[30]

Hovey came from a wealthy, liberal Boston family that could trace its American ancestry back to 1635. He had attended Harvard University, edited the *Harvard Crimson,* and been one of the first protégés of the legendary English professor Charles Townsend Copeland. When Lincoln Steffens became city editor of the *New York Commercial Advertiser* in 1897, he began replacing the older reporters with recent Harvard and Yale graduates, including two of Copeland's favorites, Hutchins Hapgood and Carl Hovey. Steffens urged them to take a less rigid view of news material and practice a literary journalism. He did not insist that they promote particular political or social themes.[31]

Steffens left the *Advertiser* for *McClure's* in 1901, but I do not know if Hovey followed. He did write two biographies, one of Stonewall Jackson (1900) and another of J. Pierpont Morgan (1911). The latter indicates that Hovey was a good writer and an objective thinker:

> this life takes Mr. Morgan neither angrily nor bitterly, nor extravagantly nor pathetically...but undertakes to describe him seriously and intelligently. ...[The biographical material]

seems to be pointing to the conclusion that Mr. Morgan's life has been one of usefulness and benefit to industry and to the country.[32]

Sonya would contribute hugely to *The Metropolitan's* reputation as a literary magazine, and she and Hovey would eventually marry and produce two children.

Chapter 2

At *The Metropolitan*

Shortly before Hovey became its co-editor (with H. J. Whigham), *The Metropolitan* had been purchased by Harry Payne Whitney, who increased the physical size of the magazine, the number of illustrations, and the length of its fiction. According to Mabel Dodge, who sponsored perhaps the most esteemed literary, artistic, and political salon in prewar Greenwich Village:

> This magazine was the most popular, and the most expensively printed and illustrated, ten-cent periodical of the day. Sonya Levien, a beautiful girl of Russian parentage, was Hovey's secretary and I always felt her judgment and her strength were a strong element in the office....Sonya had that most enduring quality: worthy weight and substance, character in short.[1]

The editors began 1912 with a radical progressive line, stating in March:

> Any progressive policy that does not have as its chief aim a redistribution of industrial profits so that the laborer may get his share, is to our way of thinking nothing more than a political dodge....The [William Jennings] Bryans and the Woodrow Wilsons and other demagogues do not burn to free the industrial laborer from his slavery; all they want to do is to keep him drugged with false hopes. Conservatives like Mr.

[President William Howard] Taft do not even know that slavery exists.[2]

As part of the editors' campaign for an activist progressivism, Hovey authored a complimentary profile of Congressman Oscar Underwood (Dem., Alabama), floor leader in the House of Representatives and a leading candidate for the party's presidential nomination. Underwood led the campaign for lower tariffs, a progressive reform designed to increase the purchasing power of workers and hence stimulate production and employment. In April, the editors endorsed Theodore Roosevelt's "new nationalism" campaign to secure the Republican nomination for president.

A few months later, the editors situated the magazine in the socialist camp. A six-part series by Morris Hillquit ("Socialism Up To Date") and an editorial signaled this shift:

> we are in fact committed [to socialism] for all the future. If we were not ourselves thoroughly imbued with the feelings and beliefs which underlie Socialism it would be childish for us to attempt to publish a thoroughly freethinking magazine.... We believe that what we call democracy has done its best—and its worst. No serious progress is possible now without a thorough readjustment of the rewards of labor, so that all men may have a chance of real life and liberty.[3]

Though the editors still preferred Roosevelt and believed his election would benefit Socialists most, they announced that Socialists "should not vote" for him—"The Socialist looks to the future; he must not be an opportunist."[4] Nor may he be violent. A September editorial announced that the magazine will "do everything in its power to foster the growth of the Socialist Party in Congress and in the state legislatures,"[5] while one the following year criticized the direct action tactics of the Industrial Workers of the World.[6] Articles by socialists Helen Keller, George D. Herron, and John Reed appeared regularly.

But *The Metropolitan* remained more renowned for its fiction, publishing works by Joseph Conrad, John Galsworthy, P. G. Wodehouse, H. H. Munro (Saki), Clarence Day, Jr., Zoë Akins, Theodore Dreiser, Rudyard Kipling, Sinclair Lewis, Anzia Yezierska, Edna Ferber, Booth Tarkington, and a new discovery, Sonya Levien. In "The Little Prophet of the Immigrants," Levien depicts an emigré from Russia, "called the Little Old Girl"—"the usual product of long years of sweated labor, starvation wages and radical thought. Thin lips and haunting eyes were the most of her, the rest belonged to the ordinary." This woman describes the plight of the immigrant worker: the awful conditions on the job and on strike; the horrors of the Triangle Shirtwaist fire; and the efforts of employers to divide workers along ethnic lines and undermine labor-union organizing. "O wasteful America!" it concludes. "We boast we are a clever people, yet go on juggling with youth and its dreams."[7]

There is no evidence to indicate that Levien belonged to any club or organization during these years. She did, however, know several Socialist Party leaders and the members of what was probably the first feminist consciousness-raising group—Heterodoxy. Founded in 1912 by Marie Jenny Howe, with twenty-five charter members of widely divergent views, it met for luncheons featuring discussions and speakers and sponsored two mass meetings in 1914 (the second entitled "What Is Feminism?"). One of its members, Charlotte Perkins Gilman, said it "was composed of various ultra-heretical thinkers, or doers, or those wishing to be so considered, which I found interesting for a while, but when the heresies seemed to center on sex psychology and pacifism, I wearied of it." Its members included Crystal Eastman, Henrietta Rodman, Rheta Childe Dorr, Inez Haynes Irwin, Mary Heaton Vorse, and Rose Pastor Stokes, all of whom Levien knew.[8]

Levien identified strongly with the woman suffrage movement. In May 1913, she sailed for England to interview a

Chicago woman jailed for militant suffrage activity, purchase fiction, and interview famous authors. She secured promises from Israel Zangwill, George Bernard Shaw (who called her "a little nuisance"), Havelock Ellis, Rudyard Kipling, and May Sinclair. She spent time with members of the Women's Suffrage Political Union and wrote a complimentary account of them and their militancy.[9]

Sonya devoted a large amount of time to the People's Institute, which attempted to link immigrants into communities and provide them with knowledge, leadership qualities, and public speaking skills. It offered a free forum for discussion of current issues (at Cooper Union), including state and municipal reform, socialism, feminism, and industrial conditions, and carried on various educational activities south of Fourteenth Street.[10] Based on one aspect of her work there, Sonya wrote an article for *The Survey* that described New York City's first civic Christmas tree and commented on the means by which a city of immigrants can build an alternative social tradition. "It can never be resurrected in any literal way, but by community action as such it can be recreated in far richer and deeper kind." She urged people to build around those holidays—Christmas, Easter, symbolic feast days—with which they had deep personal, not political or patriotic, associations, a new social tradition, community sentiment, and community life.[11]

Levien also served as Educational Secretary of the Institute's National Board of Censorship, its movie review board. In a memorandum to Frederic C. Howe, the Institute's director, she wrote: "My work consists in establishing and making permanent the Educational Department of the National Board of Censorship thru publicity, correspondence and interviews, lectures, etc." She furnished over one hundred institutions with information on the regulation of movie theaters, placed stories on the board's work, prepared and distributed pamphlets on movies, and lectured on the board's work "on the average of once a week, before commissions appointed by Mayors, Governors, etc., private organizations, organized for the regulation of motion pictures, legislative committees, churches, women's organizations, schools, etc." She also lobbied before state legislatures on behalf of motion picture regulation bills.[12] She focused not on the content of the movies shown but the environment in which they were shown.

When New York City passed a comprehensive law regulating the city's movie theaters in 1913, Levien wrote an article praising it as a "model ordinance." The motion picture, she wrote,

> is the most popular and influential of recreations, and yet it has been left entirely to the exploitation of private interests, resulting in the moral and physical detriment of the people, especially of the children. To meet the demands for motion picture entertainment, every conceivable hole of a store or hall has been converted into a "theater," with no regard whatever to the fire hazard or unwholesomeness of the place.[13]

When World War I began in August 1914, Levien was again in London, covering, and trying to become involved in, the British suffragist movement. "I pleaded with those in authority to be taken in....It was not curiosity, I urged, or lack of understanding. I believed in votes, but I believed in women more; I wanted to feel as well as understand their great Purpose." For two weeks, she immersed herself in the arena of the militant London suffragette:

> Scared and horrified, I witnessed the burning of two famous old churches; I helped in the heckling of public speakers, and remonstrated with the police at their outrages upon unoffending women.
>
> The spiritual urge of the fighting women transmitted itself to me and I found myself supporting them with a courage not natural to me. That the character of their protest might be

petty, tactless, unwomanly, or even futile, mattered not—for one felt that they were soldiers fighting in a great cause, the slogan of which was: "Give us a chance to develop a better race of men and women."

While she was there,

the cataclysm of war descended upon all Europe and civilized man went mad for murder—wholesale terrible murder without reason or purpose. Sickened by the cry for blood, the women's fight became holy in its significance to me....For the first time I felt the real greatness of the women's fight and the sad futility of it before man's ignorance. For the first time I felt the real tragedy of the women of Europe whose business it is to bring up sons for the man's *game of war*.[14]

Though a number of the women she knew became leaders in the American peace movement, forming and joining the Woman's Peace Party or the American Union Against Mobilization, there is no evidence that Levien actively opposed either the war or United States involvement in it. She did, however, pay close attention to women's groups. Commenting on the pacifistic International Congress of Women at the Hague (April-May 1915), Levien praised their motives but criticized the movement's lack of "massiveness and direction....The emotional unity of a few hundred women becomes powerless when pitted against the present uncivilization, and even were they to join hands with all the outraged motherhood of Europe it would be of little avail. Mere pacifism does not end war." Instead, they should "sacrifice all in their effort to do away with the institutions that make for war."[15]

In the next fourteen months, she wrote regular editorials commenting on the need for women to expand their aims beyond suffrage to earning equal salaries, improving their living conditions, and reforming schools, cities, and politics.

She also wrote sympathetically about workers and their struggles.

The Metropolitan's editors advocated the direct involvement of the United States in the war, but they did so in a decidedly less bellicose and nationalistic manner than most hawks, while maintaining their disdain for President Wilson's domestic policies.

> If we want to make the world safe for democracy there are two things we must surely do. First of all we must so deal with Germany that neither she nor any other great power will ever again think it worth while to start out on a career of world conquest....
>
> Second, to make democracy safe we must make democracy self-supporting. Washington at the present moment of writing is rather a deplorable spectacle.[16]

Since the Socialist Party adhered to a strong antiwar position, the editors moved toward a conservative progressivism. Their relationship with John Reed provides a reasonably accurate gauge of *The Metropolitan*'s moderating political line. Before the war, at the suggestion of Lincoln Steffens, Hovey had engaged Reed to cover the Mexican revolution from the camp of Pancho Villa, one of the revolutionary leaders. Immediately thereafter, in spring 1914, Reed covered the bloody battle at Ludlow, Colorado that pitted striking miners against gunmen hired by the Rockefeller interests. In the autumn, he was sent to report on the war in western Europe and the Balkans. But a gap had opened, and Reed began sending his best (antiwar) material to the left-wing *Masses*, while the editors hired Theodore Roosevelt as a contributing editor. Reed and Roosevelt despised each other and almost came to blows on one occasion.

Though the editors continued to use Reed on important assignments such as the national political conventions of 1916 and planned to send him to China in early 1917, Reed wrote Whigham: "You and I call ourselves friends, but we are not really friends, because we don't believe in the same things, and the time will come when we won't speak to one another." That time came in January 1917, following the United States' severing of relations with Germany. The editors cancelled the China trip and ceased to publish Reed's work. In his reminiscences, Hovey wrote:

> We could be noble, but not too noble. Could probe the sore spots of society, to take Steffens' figure [of speech], but not too deeply where it hurt....Reed had become what he wished to be, the embodiment of rebellion against the course his country had chosen to follow. The vision that hovered before his eyes—the poet's instinctive dream of a world entirely better—could not be shared...by a publication widely read and with its feet on the ground of native soil. It was fine for Reed to hate war and say so [in *Masses*]. But the magazine [*The Metropolitan*] could no longer be his platform; even if its editors saw with his eyes, which was not the case, it would merely mean the end. *The Metropolitan* would have been instantly, cheerfully, squelched.[17]

Roosevelt, on the other hand, became a significant part of the magazine, as contributor and personality. Hovey had admired him for years (had praised his presidency in the Morgan biography) and had approved Roosevelt's outrage over President Wilson's failure to prepare the United States for war. Agreeing to double what Roosevelt had received for his previous contributions to the *Outlook*—to pay him $25,000 a year—Hovey assigned Sonya as his editor. "He had," she recalled, "a vivid way of expressing himself that often did not appear in his writing. And it was decided that I should help him to put back his picturesque phrases in the articles." She adored him, even though they disagreed on a subject very close to her.

> I grew warm about the vast throngs of people who drag themselves every morning at seven to the factories, work at

some trifling job for eight, ten hours, day in, day out, year after year, without respite, without hope of ultimate release except through death. The unpleasant memories of my own similar beginnings keep ever alive for me the sordidness of such an existence. My deep resentment against an industrial order that extorts so usurious a toll from its masses did not meet with the sympathy I had expected.

Roosevelt, who called her "little miss anarchist...for no other reason that I could discover except that he knew I was born in Russia and had been brought up in a radical environment," replied that radicals like her laid too much emphasis on the drudgery of a day's work, that most work was drudgery, and that the success or failure of each person depended upon that person's own character.

On Roosevelt's death, she ranked him with George Washington and Abraham Lincoln as a president and statesman and sang his praises as an explorer, biologist, naturalist, and man of letters. "[W]hen we think of Colonel Roosevelt," she concluded, "we think of the truest citizen of a true America, a man who possessed the spirit of youth and of pioneering, who was a friend to all honest men and women, and who lived up to his convictions in his private and public life with courage and everlasting faith in humanity."[18]

Agreeing with Roosevelt, *The Metropolitan*'s editorials excoriated virtually every aspect of President Wilson's presidency and denounced the Bolshevik Revolution in Russia. By 1919, the magazine had shed most of its radicalism and become mainly a venue for fiction. For her part, Sonya maintained contacts with socialists (Crystal Eastman), labor events (Women's Trade Union League), and feminists (Inez Haynes Irwin), and later told an interviewer, "I am not a Bolshevik, yet I frankly say there is no denial of some of the things accomplished by them."[19]

Her personal life was full. She attended the theater with John Reed and Eugene O'Neill, the Evenings at Mabel Dodge's and teas at the Stokes's, lunched with Margaret

Sanger, Louise Bryant, Felix Frankfurter, Harold Laski, and Jesse Lasky. She also became interested in psychic phenomena through her friendship with writer Mary Austin. Influenced by the writings of Henri Bergson and William James, Austin wrote to Levien about the development of psychic power in the individual and psychic phenomena in the world — "a light arising out of Russia...—an organizing, revivifying light." Levien responded:

> Of course I realize how often a psychic contact can be misleading, but I can't help feeling great faith in your vision. I shall be watching with you for developments and will *almost pray* (strange for me) for its fulfillment. I want peace to come like nothing else on earth, and want it to come soon.

Austin called Levien "the guardian of my psychic adventures" and valued her interest and lack of bias.[20]

On October 11, 1917, Sonya married Carl Hovey. It had been "antagonism at first sight," she later wrote. "We worked together, however, and that made us companionable, and then we fell in love." Hovey was an Anglo-Saxon Protestant, but she had found no "romantic appeal" in the Jewish males she had known, no "race feeling" in Hovey, and a compatibility in social ideals. He was, recounted Ludwig, a tall, lean, good-looking man; a gentleman to the core; highly intelligent; a great sense of humor; a Democrat with strong liberal tendencies; a good, good person, "who looked on Sonya with a kind of benign amusement. As if he couldn't believe her. 'She's a tough broad to handle,' he once jocularly said to me."[21]

Secure in her love for him, the families' reactions worried her. At the Levien family conference on the subject, Julius said he had no objection if the children were declared Jewish (though they would be free to choose their own form of worship) and if Carl agreed to a circumcision. Sonya's brothers met with him, and he told them he was already circumcised. When they reported this news to Julius, he asked, "did you see it?" So they had to go back and visually verify that the operation had been done.[22]

Sonya told Ludwig that she had been scared to death at meeting the Hovey family, "one of the top gentile, Puritan, Plymouth-Rock, New-England, rock-ribbed families." Mrs. Hovey asked Sonya to sit beside her. "Born in Russia? Jewish?" When Sonya nervously replied in the affirmative, Mrs. Hovey responded, "That's good; it's about time we had some fresh blood in the family."

The couple lived on east 92nd Street, between Fifth and Madison avenues, with Hovey's two children from a former marriage. They had decided to declare their children Jewish but not to provide them with any religious training whatsoever. In later years, Sonya would express regret over the "inconsistency" between her religious belief and practice, and admit she felt "uneasy about the sort of [orthodox] training [her] children were missing, and which [she] had received."[23]

Another gap between belief and practice opened in her political consciousness. Though she retained a critical attitude toward political events, she ceased to write or speak about them or promote them in any significant way. She had decided, in 1918, that the United States, despite the hunger and suffering in its cities' slums, "affords opportunities for equality and democracy as no other nation in the world" and that its struggle for freedom was "untainted" compared to the histories of other countries.[24] She had become a sort of patriot and would evolve into a quiet New Deal liberal.

Her energies now focused on her writing, Sonya sent stories to *Saturday Evening Post, Collier's, Redbook, Ladies Home Journal, Harpers, Cosmopolitan, Atlantic Monthly,* and *Century, inter alia*. Clarence Day, Jr., who wrote for *The Metropolitan* and conducted its book department, strongly encouraged her efforts, and they began to critique each other's work. At one point, Day wrote, "Be brutal to me or I won't be to you!"[25]

Levien had advised aspiring writers to appeal to a large audience and hold the reader's attention. In her editorial capacity, she rejected "The slight story" (does not move one vitally), "The shop-talk story" (too narrow), "The propaganda story" (too much preaching), "The story with a sad ending," "The unconvincing story," and "The story with a foreign setting." She advised writers to "be brave at all costs," concentrate on "those subtle honesties of characterization and motive," and fearlessly and frankly to put themselves in their work.[26]

She followed her own advice, mainly composing melodramas about immigrant families, and her 1921 diary indicates that she did not enjoy enormous success in placing them. "The 14 K. Doctor" was sent to seventeen editors, "Baby Doll" to five, and two others to four each. In a letter to Day accompanying the "Baby Doll" manuscript, she worried about its lack of originality and sincerity — that she appeared too aware of what she was doing and too obviously satisfied with the final product. Day, however, thought it was "vital." "I am glad that 'it's a different part of you that writes' and I hope to God it always will be."

> I don't see how it can help be sure-fire! Why my god, it has all the stock characters in the world in it! That is, all the reliable ones, that people love. The pale coughing boy (curse him!), the beautiful sister—a flower of the slums too in this case—the 100% villain, the grouchy young rich man, they're all there, working hard for you. And you've given them several new twists. The comic relief too—the old Irishwoman.
>
> ...[T]his isn't the kind of story that *I* normally should have much appetite for, but it's a funny thing, I had a sensation now and then as I read it, that I was standing near an East Side stoop where you couldn't see me, and that you were a little girl sitting there telling a story to your friends—telling it with both hands, and with your eyes and tongue and everything else, and rushing through it and making it vivid, and fascinating....

Not only had Day accurately described the prototypical Levien style and content, he also saw its value for another medium. "If you sell all this for less than a thousand you're not a good business women, and how much the movies will give you besides, Croesus alone knows." In a more cynical vein, an editor had once told Levien, "if [you] were to write a Greek tragedy in heroic measure it would eventually land as a Mack Sennett comedy."[27]

In fact, Famous Players-Lasky purchased "Baby Doll," and it became one of Levien's first credits (original story for the movie *Top of New York*). A promising new career opened before her.[28]

Chapter 3

The Movie Industry and the Scenario Writer

When Sonya Levien began selling her stories to the motion picture industry, moviemaking was undergoing important changes. The studios were frantically dumping their inventory of war movies and projects and frenziedly replacing them with romance and adventure scenarios. As audiences flocked into the theaters, production multiplied, manuscripts poured into the studios, prices for novels and plays soared, a theater-building spree commenced, and admission prices rose markedly. Movies increased in length and cost and improved in quality.[1]

In addition, the nature of the audience changed from mainly immigrant working class to assimilated middle class. As a result, according to Lewis Jacobs, "movies had to be more subtle and refined, broader in scope, not quite so simple and forthright." They became less preachy and outwardly moralistic. "The old axioms were now disseminated indirectly, by implication and inference. Instead of sympathetically portraying the poor, films turned to disparaging the rich." Love stories increased enormously, especially the rags-to-riches romances featuring spirited and spunky young women. The "vamp" appeared on screen; polite comedy and satire replaced burlesque and slapstick.[2]

Cecil B. DeMille and his screenwriter, Jeanie Macpherson,

seeking the most attractive box-office formula, focused on "sex appeal." She wanted to move beyond the image of the sexy vamp and siren "and to broaden the scope of this ingredient to include all the subtle manifestations of feminine charm which had come into vogue after the war." Their first effort in this genre, *Male and Female* (1919), based on James M. Barrie's play, *The Admirable Crichton*, and featuring Gloria Swanson, cost $170,000 and earned $1.25 million.[3]

When Frances Marion returned to Hollywood in 1919 from her stint as a war correspondent, she discovered that producers wanted romance and love stories only.

> We writers were fed to the teeth with Love and Happy Endings. But what could we do? The bosses told us that if we wanted to write bleak realistic stories which ended unhappily we could spin our yarns for magazines or publishers of books. The movies must be heart-lifting, not eyebrow-lifting.[4]

The "social film," which revealed the various problems of a society undergoing dislocation—corruption in city politics, white slavery, exploitation of immigrants—virtually ceased to appear after 1920.[5] But the melodramatic form in which the social dramas had been encased was retained, allowing moviemakers to combine "real" experiences with satisfying endings. Recognizable and adaptable, the melodrama genre could depict all manner of social, familial, and relational situations in ways that might both entertain and edify.[6]

Rags-to-riches or "Cinderella" romances reappeared, providing a means for moviemakers to deal facilely with social-class differentiation. A lower- or working-class female stumbles into the upper-class milieu. Her values (honesty, hard work, sincerity) prove superior to the conduct of the upper-class male and his family (who are irresponsible and pretentious). But she spends sufficient time in his environment—they must, after all, meet, fight, captivate, separate, and reunite—to allow the movie to display all the glittery objects that money can buy. This light-comedy format replaced the physical comedy of the two-reelers, giving writers the opportunity to depict more believable situations and characters and directors the opportunity to replace title cards with more sophisticated visual depictions.

The structure of the industry also underwent major changes that placed tighter restraints on story content. The two largest employers, Paramount and Universal, found that the enormous increase in production rendered it impossible for one person to oversee all the projects. At Paramount, for example, Jesse L. Lasky created a new kind of executive to oversee writing and production of individual pictures — "supervisors."[7] At Universal and then at M-G-M, Irving Thalberg would refine this system of studio producers to its peak of efficiency.

In 1922, industry owners, fearing the effect of scandals and unrestrained use of sexy topics, instituted a scheme of self-regulation and self-censorship in the form of the Motion Picture Producers and Distributors of America and appointed former Postmaster General Will H. Hays as president and chief keeper of the moral flame. According to Marion, the Hays office severely restricted scenarists. "They dared not write frankly about any vital issue, but were forced to turn out sugarcoated yarns."[8]

The Scenario Writer

As movies increased in expense, length, and complexity, the scenario's value soared. It could, if adapted from a successful novel, play, or story, carry a presold value; it allowed the executives to predict and to some degree control costs. Therefore, the method of securing properties and adapters of these properties became better organized.

Prior to 1920, most writers came to the movie studios from newspapers or popular fiction. The trade journal *Motography* indicated (September 1916) that newspaper people "know life, a good story, and the value of a gripping situation."[9] Those writers who could make the transition, adapting their writing to the motion picture craft, were not all that prevalent. When those with such skills surfaced, studio supervisors wanted to keep them, so the contract writer, whose entire movie story product was owned by the studio that employed him or her, began to replace the free-lancer and speculator. In 1919, Lasky told Adolph Zukor:

> We've got to break the bottleneck in the story department.... We can't rely any longer on simply sifting what comes to us spontaneously. We must begin actively to stimulate the creative literary processes. We've got to increase the supply of top-quality screen material and control some of the sources for our own protection.

Lasky wanted either to sign top playwrights and novelists to studio contracts or purchase a large Broadway production company with a large backlog of plays.[10]

That same year, Samuel Goldwyn formed Eminent Authors Pictures with seven well-known novelists. According to Benjamin Hampton:

> Prior to 1919-20, the screen rights of novels and plays had been purchasable at a thousand to ten thousand dollars. In later years, producers have paid a thousand, five thousand, and ten thousand dollars for the right to adapt a magazine story, and novelists have received $25,000 to $100,000 for popular books. Successful plays have brought as high as $225,000.[11]

Scenario writers' salaries advanced apace. At the high end, valued contract writers could receive upwards of $1,000 a week or flat fees of $10,000 to $25,000 to write and script a story for the screen or adapt an expensive novel or play. Title writers became a specialized, highly paid profession as well.[12]

Their product, the "continuity" script, was firmly set in place by 1920, and articles in trade papers and a variety of handbooks helped standardize its format on an industry-wide basis.[13] Kenneth Macgowan credited C. Gardner Sullivan and Thomas H. Ince with creating the continuity method.

> The action is pared down to the bone and then fleshed with exact and appropriate details. The film is started easily and naturally with the introduction of a character or two and an emotion and a place, which gradually begin to accumulate action—and interest—about them....Life just begins to live before you. As you go forward with the story, the effect is of a taut and clean-cut structure designed to achieve the strongest possible dramatic effect....The story is always arranged so as to flow as much as possible without [the help of descriptive subtitles]....[T]he Sullivan dramaturgy is, after all, not unlike the [Henrik] Ibsen dramaturgy in its definite, tight structure.

Macgowan strongly opposed the practice of filming plays and adapting novels with scrupulous fidelity. He threatened "a severe penalty for any continuity writer who doesn't throw overboard three-fifths of any novel."[14]

Bayard Veiller, a playwright named to head Metro's scenario staff, even though he had seen less than twelve movies in his life and did not know "a continuity from a fishing-pole," believed that the basic principle of scenario writing was "arousing and holding your audience's interest."[15] The unspoken qualifier, "by any means necessary," marked the eternal divide between writer and showman. Benjamin Hampton, who worked in the executive ranks of the industry from 1916-26, believed that screenwriters were a "class" of people who, "with few exceptions were apt to concentrate their efforts on the intelligent minority of movie audiences....[T]hey too often spend their employer's money to win the applause of intellectuals, neglecting the populace that in the long run pays for everything."[16]

Rupert Hughes, speaking for the Eminent Authors, argued

that the only way to reach a movie audience "is with sincerity"; movies "must appeal to the audience as real." But, he continued,

> at the present time, pictures are turned out, in the main, like so many sausages. The scenario editor says we must have a little thrill, a little love, a little villainy and a final clinch. He takes all ideas, all stories and forces them thru [sic] the same mould. Logic has nothing whatever to do with it.
> ...[F]ilm companies pay thousands and thousands of dollars for some story or novel by a well-known author, and, when it has gone thru the scenario editor's hands, no author would recognize his own story. [Because] it is a scenario editor's religion that a story-teller could never write anything wholly suited for the screen. The scenario writer makes no effort to understand the theme of the original story, but thrusts it thru the conventional actions.[17]

The truth of writing for the screen falls somewhere in between Veiller/Hampton and Hughes. As William C. de Mille noted, "Just now the average photoplay writer is not good enough, while the good enough writer is not competent in his new trade [photoplay writing]." Writers were only in the early stages of acquiring the skills to craft their literary language (original stories or adaptations) into film language. The relation between literal and visual elements, between words and pictures, remained in a "nebular state."[18]

Shortly after he came to the industry, Carl Hovey commented that screen stories were the weakest element in the moviemaking process. The studios were loaded with people highly gifted in every other phase of the process, he wrote, but only a handful of people were "gifted with the ability to tell a story." Although he mentioned a number of movies that displayed a freshness of approach, only *The Big Parade* received his wholehearted praise for sincere, natural, human handling of its story material.[19]

The advent of sound in the late 1920s altered the scenario-writing constituency. Dialogue writing became the rage, and production heads stripped their payrolls of gag and title writers, retaining only the most-trusted constructionists and pairing them with imports from the theater—anyone with a track record of writing "lines." From this mating of constructionist and dialoguer emerged the screenwriter of the studio era.

The Screenwriter

Few final shooting scripts in the studio era came from the pen or typewriter of one writer. The vast majority of scripts, produced and unproduced, resulted from the collaboration of anywhere from four to fourteen writers. Kenneth Macgowan recalled:

> When I was producing thirty features at Twentieth-Century Fox between 1935 and 1943, I supervised the writing on fifty-two stories that were never produced. At least ninety writers worked on these abortive assignments....Of the thirty features actually produced, two-thirds had more than one collaborator. On a quarter of them, six to eleven writers were involved between the first outline and the final shooting script.

He could remember only two that could be credited to a single writer. At M-G-M during the late 1930s, each script averaged seven writers.[20]

Most heads of production and supervising producers believed that screenplays were edited, not written. All the available evidence—story conference notes, studio memos, and memoirs—indicate that the producer class was convinced that its members alone possessed the secret of refining entertainment from the raw ore handed to it by the screenwriter class. F. Scott Fitzgerald, who apprenticed long and hard at the screenwriting craft, had his fictional production head, Monroe Stahr, say "we put them on an idea in pairs, and if it slows down, we put two more writers working behind them. I've had as many as three pairs working independently on the same idea." But where is the unity, he is asked. "I'm the unity," he replied.[21] Donald Ogden Stewart recalled that during the 1930s "the competition was very great—you couldn't make mistakes because there were other writers waiting to step in and fix your script up the way you were fixing somebody else's."[22]

The standard writer's contract made it clear that all written material "shall automatically become our [studio's] property, and for this purpose, we shall be deemed to be the author thereof." In other words, individual writers became part of a corporate authorship, an employee engaged in the production of a commodity, no longer a freely creative or expressive artist. Leo Rosten concluded:

> It is significant that the writers who find it easiest to adjust to Hollywood are (1) writers who have served as writer-employees before coming to Hollywood (newspapermen, advertising writers, publicists), (2) writers who have written only for the screen. These men do not invest too much self-esteem in their work....They accept the *conditions* of screen writing as well as the weekly checks, and recognize the necessary conjunction of the two.[23]

According to Lester Cole, who worked regularly from the early 1930s until his blacklisting in 1947, "my gratification comes from the fact that I have in some way endeavored to put forth truthfully and well certain things about people engaged in whatever dramatic action there is. I don't expect [the audience] to see that work and relate it to me personally."[24]

The successful screenwriter received a very high salary. Between 1931-33, the annual compensation of the regularly employed writer averaged slightly less than $14,000. Irregularly employed writers averaged $3,300. By 1939, the median weekly wage was $120. Probably about 10 percent of the screenwriting population produced the bulk of the final shooting scripts. They could expect to earn upwards of $500 a week when they worked, but employment could be irregular. In 1941, five screenwriters earned more than $75,000 (out of an industry list of over 200 earning that much or more): Jo Swerling, $97,500, James K. McGuiness, $91,875, Anita Loos, $88,375, John Lee Mahin, $79,166, and Virginia Van Upp, $75,800.[25]

In sum, screenwriters were tightly controlled by contracts and supervisors, wrote much more material than could be produced, were frequently typecast and regularly rewritten, and were deemed much less important than directors or stars. They relinquished, as well, the traditional notion of authorship and the process of creativity and had to agree to produce entertaining—not literary or aesthetic—scripts from properties that frequently lacked any cinematic value. On the other hand, they did not have to worry about selling their final products; they were not held responsible if the movie failed; and many earned far higher salaries than they could have elsewhere.

Lured by the money, the mystique of filmed storytelling, and the vast movie audience, many aspired, but only a relatively small percentage mastered the unique skills of movie writing. However frustrated they were by the studio system, most screenwriters possessed the heart of an artisan, and very few wrote less than their best. Contrary to legend, the script-writing process did not suck the creative juices from a writer. Those with the requisite will and discipline wrote books and plays.

Female Writers

At the center of the changes occurring in the motion picture industry from 1915-27 (the Jazz Age), writes Gerald Mast, "was the new American woman—or, rather, women. The many new types of women on movie screens indicated the conflicting varieties of experience in modern American life."[26] Making movies was among these experiences, and women were among the forerunners in developing the screenwriting technique. Anita Loos, for example, is credited with melding the best of Broadway dialogue writing with visual scenarios. She and her husband-collaborator, John Emerson, wrote two books on the craft, stressing in both that scenario writing is a lucrative writing profession not requiring unusual genius but only "a dramatic insight and certain amount of training." The would-be scenario writer needed "[o]riginality, a sense of humor, experience in any form of writing—as newspaper work or fiction—time and determination to write stories."[27] They did not specify that women could apply; they took that as a given.

According to Anthony Slide, women "might be said to have virtually controlled the film industry" during the silent movie era. They were the bankable stars; there were more than thirty women directors and nearly fifty women writers; and some women formed independent production companies.[28] In her compilation of 100 noted screen people of 1920, Carolyn Lowrey highlights 36 women: 29 actresses, 4 writers, 1 director, and 2 producers. Some were hyphenates, filling several roles. Actress Leah Baird wrote scenarios, and actress Virginia Pearson formed her own production company. Lois Weber wrote, acted, and edited before becoming a director. As a director, she wrote most of her own scenarios and co-produced them with her husband. Jeanie Macpherson wrote, acted, and directed before Cecil B. DeMille hired her strictly as a writer. And June Mathis headed Metro's scenario department, watching "the filming, cutting and titling of each production, lending aid wherever she may."[29] Perhaps the most omnicompetent of them all, Nell Shipman, acted, wrote, directed, and founded her own production companies.[30] Ally Acker argues that these women did not think of themselves as "women directors" or "women scenarists." Gender, she thinks, "never entered their consciousness." Well educated, ambitious, absorbed in movies, they saw themselves as "outsiders," different than other men and women.[31]

It is simply impossible, at this point, to declare with any precision how many women wrote scenarios for silent movies and how many scenarios they wrote. Anecdotal evidence indicates that a higher proportion of women wrote a higher proportion of scenarios in the silent period than they did in the sound era. Though a handful of women made the transition, again anecdotal evidence suggests that the greater number fell by the wayside. When asked why, Lenore Coffee, one of those who flourished in both epochs, commented, "A silent film was like writing a novel, and a script was like writing a play. That's why women dropped out. Women had been good novelists, but in talking pictures women were not predominant," because there were few prominent female playwrights.[32]

Frances Marion basically agreed, noting that "producers immediately got the idea that unless you had written a stage play, you could not possibly write for actors transformed overnight into marathon talkers. They sent an S.O.S. across the country to round up any man or woman who had ever put his line on paper under the label 'Dialogue.'" But, she continued, these "dialogue writers," unaccustomed to the swifter pace required by movie scenarios, wrote unsatisfactory, static scripts. "Baffled, the producers finally permitted the scenarists to become humble assistants to these dialogue writers. We did not relish the chore, but obeyed implicitly, our eyes on our paychecks."[33]

The compilation *Who Wrote the Movie...?* lists about 2,800 writers for the period 1929-60. Less than 10 percent (216) are women, and only 130 of these had five or more career credits. Sonya Levien easily tops the list of "A" credits; most of the women with numbers approaching hers wrote "B" westerns. Female screenwriters received less than 10 percent of the nominations for Academy Awards (53/600) and Oscars

(9/119). They did slightly better in the Guild award categories.[34]

Of course, women who wanted to write movies in the early years of the industry did not consider gender percentages. Entering the industry in its fetal phase simply meant pleasing a director with one's ideas. Nell Shipman (1892-1970) recalled:

> In the lapse of time between stage and screen [acting], I learned to write scenarios. My first one got a prize. The following dozen did not. I wrote the first picture to be produced in Australia and spent a month in the New York Public Library getting "atmosphere." "Under the Crescent," which appeared as a book, a serial, and a song took two months' study. During this "literary" period I became interested in "Feminism," "Socialism," and other "Isms." I wrote constantly, short stories, sketches, articles, poems, scenarios, and so forth.[35]

Anita Loos (1893-1981) was a stage actress who, after seeing her first movie and realizing that films require plots, "decided to try my hand at writing one. I worked it out the next morning and arrived early at rehearsal in order to climb up into the projection booth and search a film can for an address where I might send my story." She sent *The New York Hat* to Biograph Company under the name A. Loos, "which I thought would make me appear to be a man and a more seasoned author." Receiving $25 for it and bored with her acting job, she continued to write film plots. "The majority were slapstick comedies that ended in a chase by Keystone Kops." She sent one or two a month to Biograph, now signing her full name to them. When the studio moved west, she was called in for an interview. D. W. Griffith offered to use her as an actress, but she declined. "I adored finding myself in the haphazard situation of real life, where I could make up my own on-the-spot dialogue." Between 1912-15, she wrote 105 plots, of which 101 were filmed by Biograph.[36]

Frances Marion (1887-1973) had been a newspaper reporter, writer of magazine articles, and advertising artist. She became smitten with movies after meeting Mary Pickford. Hired by Lois Weber in 1913, she "skittered around [Bosworth] studio doing every kind of job I could find except emptying the garbage pails." One day, Weber handed her a shooting script and assigned her to prompt the extras. "You'll be in costume and move among them. But your principal job is to write snatches of dialogue." Slowly she evolved into a writer, and, following the sale of a scenario for Pickford, to Paramount for $125, she sent a letter to studio heads, telling them: "To prove my value as a scenarist, I'm willing to work two weeks for nothing. At the end of that time, if the results are satisfactory, I will consider a year's contract at $200 a week." Since the highest weekly rate was $75, she was not inundated with offers. William Fox offered her $80 after telling her that "nobody cares nothing about female writers. Actresses—yes, they got glamour—but writers, the poor schlemiels!" William Brady (World Film Co.) accepted her two-week free offer, and she impressed him by taking an unreleased picture off the shelf and converting it into a comedy with a new set of subtitles. After several months, she wrote *Poor Little Rich Girl* for Pickford and became her permanent scenario writer (at Paramount).[37]

Lenore Coffee (1900-84) began her professional life in advertising in San Francisco. An inveterate movie watcher, she read a story about Clara Kimball Young's need for scenarios. She wrote one, sent it to Garson Studio, and received $100 for it. A few months later, in March 1919, Harry Garson offered her $50 a week. Just before Coffee arrived in Hollywood, Garson left for New York, and she secured a job with Louis B. Mayer "to read all the material he was considering and then go in and tell the stories to his stars and convince them that they should make the picture." When Garson returned eight weeks later, he paid her back salary and put her to work. "[H]e suggested that I make notes during the shooting so that

I would feel that I was part of the production. I ended not only doing that but by reading all the fan mail, all the submitted original stories, making cutting notes, writing titles." When Garson left Hollywood to seek refinancing for his studio, she decided to establish herself as a script doctor, becoming, in her words, "a fanatic on the subject of structure." She worked for Metro, Ince, Mayer again, DeMille, and M-G-M.[38]

The de Mille/DeMille brothers seemed to prefer female screenwriters. William even married one, Clara Beranger (1886-1956), who had begun her writing life on newspapers and magazines. Jeanie Macpherson (1897-1946) wrote the vast bulk of Cecil's movies. "Amid the chorus of yes-men, flatterers and disciples, [Macpherson] alone had dared to disagree," wrote Dorothy Calhoun. William hired playwright Marion Fairfax, who was shocked at the notion that pictures were written. He "took me in hand and little by little built up in my mind a conception of what a picture might be."[39] Beulah Marie Dix (1876-1970), Lenore Coffee, and Sonya Levien also wrote for Cecil.

These women, and Jane Murfin (1893-1955), June Mathis (1892-1927), Grace Cunard (1893-1967), and Gene Gauntier (1891-1966), *inter alia*, wrote thousands of silent scenarios, and many of them continued to write during the sound era, forming the highly paid backbone of Fox and M-G-M studios. They did not see themselves as pathbreaking women; they possessed the consciousness of highly skilled craftspeople. Frances Marion recalled their reaction to Goldwyn's Eminent Authors:

> All of us who had been schooled in writing directly for the screen grew a little fearful of being undermined by so much talent, yet we knew that sooner or later these authors would find out that the screen was not an easy medium to write for. It entailed many special aspects of which they could have no previous knowledge.[40]

The Movie Industry and the Scenario Writer 47

Foreign to them was the recollection of a sound-generation female writer, Dorothy Parker, who, when asked about her Hollywood experience, replied, "I can't talk about Hollywood. It was a horror to me when I was there and it's a horror to look back on. I can't imagine how I did it. When I got away from it I couldn't even refer to the place by name. 'Out there,' I called it."[41]

William Ludwig, looking back on his decades in the industry, does not think that women writers received different treatment than men. "If they [women] delivered good scripts, they were treated as good writers. They [producers] did not ask if it was a woman or a man [writer]—[but] what was the last credit? Was it any good? How did it do [at the box office]? Nobody asked you to take your pants down." Samuel Goldwyn, Jr., also perceived successful screenwriters as genderless:

> As a woman you were an actress, a writer, or nobody. At the parties, men talked business at one end of the room, women talked their talk at the other—wives, that is. The women in the business—Frances Marion, Sonya Levien, Anita Loos—were free to roam.[42]

Bess Taffel, who wrote scripts for Paramount, Goldwyn, RKO, and Twentieth from 1942-1951, perceived studio gender relationships differently. "Of course, it made a difference that I was a woman." Some men would not work with her because they felt it inhibited the language they could use. Some men believed women writers could only write "women's movies." She had to deal with sexual overtures and, at the beginning of her career, when she was working with a male collaborator, she heard rumors that he was doing the work and she was providing the sex. "I was," she recalled, "very much aware of a man's hating to be bested by me. To feel lesser than I. I did what I could to avoid that happening or making it seem as though it were." Nor did men take a protective attitude toward her. She felt very much on her own.

There also existed, Taffel said, a widespread attitude that women could be more easily manipulated on credits. In fact, at the beginning of her career, she signed her scripts B. Taffel, to disguise her gender from the readers. But in the studio, she refused to dress or behave manishly. She wore very feminine clothes, including a bow in her hair, and refused to tell dirty jokes. Usually the only woman at the writers' table, she gracefully accepted the men acting out exaggerated gentlemanly roles.

More women did not attempt to become screenwriters, Taffel believes, because it seemed to be a man's field, complete with a gate and a sign reading "for men only." She does not think that women tried very hard to break through that gate. Her own entry was accidental. An actress, she met an aspiring writer, Ben Barzman, who told her his story problems on their dates. Finding solutions seemed like a game to her, and when she offered a story idea, he asked her to collaborate with him in writing it. Enjoying the process and meeting with success, she forged her screenwriting career.

As with Levien, Taffel did not consciously write about women breaking through or striving for equality. She was not, in her estimation, a gender-conscious writer. She wrote very few originals (working mainly on rewriting other scripts) and she, like all writers, had to write to order.

Nor did Taffel find much gender-consciousness among women in or around the industry. They did not practice solidarity or sisterhood. On the contrary, they were very competitive with one another, and Taffel also remembers the jealousy and envy radiating from some writers' wives.[43]

Moviemakers did not seem to believe that a woman writer was required to add a "woman's touch" to a movie. Indeed, George Cukor is one of the few successful sound-era directors who worked extensively with women writers. Approximately 60 percent of his movies have a female screenwriter credit attached (Jane Murfin, Adela Rogers St. John, Anita Loos, Frances Marion, Zoë Akins, Salka Viertel, and Sonya Levien). According to one of his biographers, Cukor used them, "in part, to ensure the truthfulness of the female characterizations—even, in contemporary terms, to see that the women in his films were as strong and self-reliant as possible." He regularly sent scripts to his friend Stella Bloch, asking her if they contained material demeaning to women. He was, she said, "very sympathetic, and seemed very ready to accept my objections."[44]

This, then, was the world which Sonya Levien entered temporarily in 1921, then permanently in 1925. During the course of her career, she commented extensively on the craft and industry. "I have heard," she wrote after her first tenure in Hollywood,

> of the great difficulty of breaking into the movies. That's not it. The great difficulty is staying in them. I fell in almost unawares, and the brine is still in my lungs. I am not yet certain whether I shall swim to shore or drown. One thing I am sure of, the waters are turbulent, and for the writer there are no sails or even water-wings to help him to safety. A movie queen once enthroned has quiet reigning for a few years anyway. The writer must make good with every idea—and a brilliant one is demanded of him every few hours.

She found the effort extremely taxing. "I never knew what work meant (although I have been a wage-slave for years) until I hit the motion picture profession. The over Lords pay well but demand every ounce of flesh and blood."

Hollywood is not, she continued, the best environment for "Great Authors." "The fact of the matter is that the novelist's art is one concerned with words, and the motion picture is primarily the art of pantomime, and under the most propitious circumstances the two arts mix about as easily as oil and water." Indeed, she advised those authors who sold their novels to the studios to do themselves a favor and avoid seeing the results of the continuity process—the translation of "the tender emotions and precious descriptions of the novelist" into the nuts and bolts of a scenario.

If an author wants to adapt his writings to the screen, he or she "must be prepared to go through a long and gruelling apprenticeship in technicalities that detract from the inspiration of his product and yet are essential details in screening a story." But should they become skilled in adaptation or learn to write original material directly for the screen, they will still remain tied by the contradictions of a litterateur in a commercial pictorial environment. They "are usually told that above all else, what is needed most in motion pictures, is the original and the new sort of thing. Then they are warned to include in their story all those elements that have earned other stories good box office receipts." If their final product is accepted, "always begrudgingly and without praise," their travail has just begun, because now—when they are preparing the story for the screen, writing the continuity—they have to deal with directors, stars, supervising directors, and exhibitors.

> And let me tell you that these gentlemen are Omnipotent. They can tell you how rotten your story is without even reading it. In a few minutes they will show you the drama you missed, the comedy you omitted, the human touches you overlooked, and above all else the breath-holding, dynamic, internationally important touch of real honest-to-goodness *Life* you completely forgot to include in your story in order to make it a big enough yarn for one of their Stupendous Superhuman Specials.

Her first tenure left her bitter toward the director. She advised writers to "milk him dry of all his little bright ideas and put them into your yarn to save yourself the trouble, and if he hasn't any, as is often the case, then insinuate your own bright ideas and make him believe they are his." Since it is the director "who finally lays the Golden Egg" in the movie industry, "this Arrogant Animal must be given his way or the goose will lay a rotten egg."

Given all these negatives, what keeps a writer in Hollywood? According to Levien, it is the finished product. "The rare and great moments are to see one's words, scenes, emotions, visualized on the sets....And then comes the egotistical thought 'And several million people will also see and be thrilled.' We hope so, anyhow."[45]

One decade later, Levien returned to the subject of the career screenwriter in her contribution to a book on career opportunities for women. She and 158 other women, including Margaret Bourke-White, Helena Rubinstein, Aline Bernstein, and Frances Perkins, outlined the career possibilities in ten areas ranging from agriculture to social work. Levien advised female aspirants that "special training before entering is not nearly so important as quickness to learn after you are once in....The real qualification is an ability to write....An instinct for story-telling and dramatic construction is absolutely necessary."

It is a demanding and frequently personally frustrating experience, because screenwriters are "part of a ponderous moving machine....There is nothing in the screenwriting profession for a woman who wants a quiet, peaceful life or for a writer who is ambitious for literary fame." But if a woman is a good writer, she "has as good a chance as a man to become a successful screenwriter. Her sex creates no awkwardness or difficulty. She has always been a familiar figure in the screen ranks."[46]

In fact, Levien had relatively little difficulty in finding regular work, but in spite of her success and facility, she never was self-satisfied about her craft. At the height of her career, Levien confided to her friend, Mabel Dodge Luhan: "The beginning of a picture is always tortuous to me. Getting to know my characters. Often it is not until I've finished that I really know them—and wish I had to do it all over again. The robot feeling is always there at the start."[47]

Levien was probably drawn to the movie industry because the studios offered her a readier, more remunerative market for her writing than did magazines and newspapers. The sacrifices a scenario career required—writing to order, long hours, anonymity—were no problem for a former fiction editor. She knew how to make herself and her work pleasing; she knew how to avoid making waves.

Chapter 4

Early Scenario Career

"I got into the movies," Levien said, "by trying to write serious stories for highbrow publications. They invariably got a hearing on the screen instead."[1] Starting in 1918, studios began to buy her stories about the romantic trials and tribulations of immigrant daughters. She received her first credit for original story in January 1919. In *Who Will Marry Me?"* (Bluebird Photoplays), Rosie, an immigrant Italian girl, flees an arranged marriage and moves into a settlement house. A rich young drunk proposes and then reneges. When he protects a former girlfriend by assuming the blame for a murder he did not commit, Rosie, convinced of his moral worth, in turn lies to save him from prison. They marry.

Levien received her second credit, for additional story, when Universal remade *Heart of a Jewess,* entitling it *Cheated Love.* Released in May 1921, it tells the story of Sonya, a Jewish immigrant who is loved by a settlement worker but is in love with a doctor. She works in a Yiddish theater to help the doctor advance, but he marries a wealthy heiress. One night the theater boiler explodes; she calms the panicky audience; the settlement worker rescues her; they marry. *Moving Picture World* (May 28, 1921) commented favorably on "the careful selection of topics to interpret the story," and *Motion Picture News* (May 28) termed it "a slice of life as it is lived in New York's teeming East Side."

In 1921, Famous Players-Lasky, the producing department

of Paramount Pictures Corp., purchased two stories from her, paying $2,500 for "The Heart of Youth" and $3,000 for "Baby Doll." The former, a story about a factory girl loving and supporting the "wrong man," received a scathing report from a studio reader—"This is trash and is utterly worthless"[2] —but became the basis for *First Love. Motion Picture News* (January 28, 1922), noting that the movie was based on Levien's story, found the movie "thoroughly clean. It embodies many human touches." *Variety* (January 6), on the other hand, called it a conventional story "convincingly pictorialized—that is, convincingly for the proletariat."

"Baby Doll," a badly written effort in search of style and wit, tried to depict the effects of the gentrification of Sutton Place and the sexual vulnerability of a young working girl supporting her family (a crippled brother and maiden aunt). Again, despite another scathing reader review—"In every respect, this a dated, tear-jerking melodrama"[3] —it was adapted for the screen under the title *The Top of New York*. It received pallid reviews as a stereotypical and old-fashioned effort. The New York *Morning Telegraph* (June 6, 1922) wrote: "Sonya Levien, from whose story 'The Top of New York' was made, and the people who made it must be steadfast believers in the tried and true. [It] has been assembled like a Ford car out of standardized parts."

Apparently pleased with her ability to write stories for the screen, Famous Players-Lasky signed Sonya to a contract. She would be paid $24,000 the first year, with annual increases of $5,000 over the next five years. Leaving husband and young son (Serge, b. 1920) behind, Levien later wrote:

> When I was given my railroad ticket I went west with something of the spirit of a modern crusader. I do not mean I went to Hollywood to improve the movies. I am neither a reformer nor a hypocrite. My whole intention was to improve myself. My dreams were avaricious and consisted of a low racing car... ; of so many glad rags....
>
> But the truth of the matter is, that I was never a movie fan.

Before I got into the profession I had dragged myself to about half a dozen in as many years. I am one of those unique creatures who never saw *The Birth of a Nation.*[4]

She told another interviewer, who asked her opinion of movies as art, "I know nothing about it at all. I am only concerned with the story I am writing at the moment."[5]

During her first Hollywood sojourn, she received credits for three adventure/romances, convoluted, farfetched tales of damsels in various types of distress. *Pink Gods* was premised on the conceit that women possessed a pathological passion for diamonds. In *The Snow Bride,* true love triumphed over evil machinations. The best of the trio, *The Exciters,* depicts the entanglement of an heiress and an undercover agent posing as a member of a gang of robbers. Only the latter scored well with critics and at the box office (foreign and domestic sales totaled $378,000 as compared to a negative cost of $216,000).[6]

Sonya's success did not compensate for her loneliness. She sorely missed her family and did not have the time, energy, or confidence to find a surrogate family in the writers' subculture. She worked well past quitting time on her scripts. "I found that all the imagination I had was needed to get my stories across on the screen." She also wanted another child and feared she might become too inured to a screen writer's salary to break away in the future. In 1923, she decided

> no money could compensate for being separated from my family. Little Serge was lonely for his mummy, and his mummy was more lonely for little Serge. I could not bring my family to the coast. My husband's work was just as important as mine and besides, a woman has no right to interfere with her husband's work—so I turned my back on Hollywood and came back home.

Because the studios did not give leaves of absence, she had to break her contract with Famous Players-Lasky.[7]

Though her return was conventional in one respect—her refusal to ask her husband to alter his career—Levien did not intend to become a housewife and mother. "I can not cook, nor sew. I am very stupid about things like that," she told an interviewer. "But I am domestic. I love my home; I love to make homes." She did not, however, wish to spend her days in them.

> There are some advantages to a mother in not being with her children every minute of the day. I'm a holiday to them, received with shouts of joy. And they're a treat to me—even more so than if I had all the tiring duties that go with the care of children and yet that do not necessarily draw mother and child closer together—the washing of little clothes, the cooking of food.[8]

Shortly after her return, she gave birth to a daughter, Tamara, and took an editorial position at *McClure's Magazine*. At some point, probably in the fall of 1924, Famous Players-Lasky asked her to adapt a novel, *Salome of the Tenements*, written by Anzia Yezierska. Yezierska, whose early life closely paralleled Levien's, had had a much different experience with Hollywood.

Born in Polotsk (ninety miles from Dvinsk) around 1883, Yezierska came to New York around 1890. She received a degree in domestic science from Teacher's College, taught school, contemplated a career as an actress, married, gave birth to a daughter, and then began to write. In 1917, she formed a close relationship with John Dewey, who encouraged her writing. Rose Pastor Stokes, with whom Yezierska shared socialist sympathies, put Yezierska in touch with Levien, who bought several of her stories for *The Metropolitan*, including a portion of *Salome*. Their publication made Yezierska a known quantity. In 1921, following the publication of a collection of her short stories about life on the Lower East Side, *Hungry Hearts*, Samuel Goldwyn paid Yezierska

$10,000 for the movie rights and invited her to write the scenario in Hollywood for $200 a week.[9]

Hungry Hearts is a collection of ten unrelated stories linked by their pitiless examination of material conditions on the Lower East Side and the emotional intensity of the female characters—their drive to survive and rise. "The Lost Beautifulness" served as the nucleus of the movie. It tells the story of a poor woman who scrimps and saves to purchase paint for her kitchen. It so improves the look of the apartment that her landlord raises the rent $5. Scrimping and cadging, she barely manages to pay it, and then he raises it another $5, telling her, "If you can't pay, somebody else will. I got to look out for myself. In America, everybody looks out for himself." Unable to pay the second increase, she is evicted, but before leaving, "with savage fury, she seized the chopping-axe" and destroyed the paint job.

In Hollywood, Yezierska was at first dazzled and overwhelmed by the luxury in which she was swaddled, and then scandalized by the caste structure. "Don't you love it out here?" she asked her secretary. "Love it! When they don't pay me enough to live?" she replied. Shaken by this display of bitterness, Yezierska met other white-collar workers, "horribly underpaid," drudging "from morning till night for less than their bread. Like a ghost at a feast, my secretary, and behind her the whole army of underdogs at the studio, rose up before me every time I stepped into the limousine. There was no peace for me at my hotel." Yezierska left Hollywood, she says, "a tortured soul with a bank account."[10]

Her account of her four-week writing effort and that of the studio vary considerably. Yezierska believed that she and her co-scenarist, Julian Josephson, had constructed a script without a false note and the studio betrayed them by hiring Montague Glass to add laughs and a happy ending. Wrote Yezierska,

> This man, with his beaming kindliness, turned out his carica-

tures of Jews like sausage meat for the popular weekly and monthly magazines. Americans read his Potash and Perlmutter stories and thought those clowning cloak and suiters were the Jewish people....My book is my life....I'll not let them murder it with slapstick.

Josephson's response, his "unbeaten calm," disappointed her. "How can you let them get away with it?" she asked.

> "Let them? I can't stop them—and I'm not crazy enough to try.
> "Screaming and yelling won't help. You've signed the contract that they can adapt the story as they think best. You were lucky that they used as much of your story as they did."
> So this was the price of my sudden riches! For forging a check, you went to prison. For forging the truth, you sat with the famous of the hour and as long as the publicity bolstered you, you'd stay there.

According to the studio's records, however, Yezierska had written a massive story outline for a twenty-reel movie, when five was the norm. Josephson had then carved a continuity script from the outline, and Glass had added titles. Abraham Lehr, the head of production, sent Yezierska Josephson's continuity for her comments and asked her advice on casting the mother, but he refused to allow her to return to Hollywood for the shooting. "Don't want Yezierska as aside from her being a hindrance to [the director, E. Mason Hopper] she will make impossible a sane shooting schedule."

The finished product, combining the painting episode with the sweatshop experiences of other Yezierska characters, horrified the author and did not please critics. The *New York Times* (November 27, 1922) reviewer called it

> a tedious recital of the sufferings of a Russian Jewish family, which may be literally exact in places but is seldom vivified by any illuminating flash of truer reality, and it proceeds from

this high point through a mass of sentimentality to an incredible and mushy ending.

Variety's (December 1) reviewer was equally critical, finding it "a thin human interest story....entirely devoid of dramatic action."

Viewing it some sixty years later, Kevin Brownlow rated it "one of the best, albeit one of the simplest, Jewish pictures of the entire silent period," though he acknowledges that it

> smoothed away all the underlying anger and all the hints of Yezierska's socialism. Gone is the wretchedness of the girl in the ghetto, her agitation for higher pay in the shirt factory, the passiveness of the other workers, and her subsequent despair.[11]

Yezierska rejected contract offers from Goldwyn and William Fox for her future work, but two years later sold her recently published novel, *Salome of the Tenements*, to Famous Players-Lasky for $7,500. The "Salome," Sonya Vrunsky, is a composite of the experiences of Yezierska (with John Dewey) and Rose Pastor (with Graham Stokes). Frantic to rise above her ghetto situation, Sonya meets John Manning, a wealthy philanthropist who has established a settlement house on the Lower East Side. Though she dislikes the ambience at the settlement house, she takes a job as Manning's secretary.

> Where else can a poor girl like me meet her millionaire if not in the settlement?...How did Rose Pastor catch on to Graham Stokes? How did Mary Antin get her chance to climb higher up? How did Sonya Levien, a plain stenographer, rise to be one of the biggest editors?

Convinced that she is in love with Manning, she eagerly accepts a lunch invitation from him. She tells herself "I'll rob, steal or murder if I got to—for clothes to make myself more beautiful for him." She convinces the great designer Jacques

Hollins (aka Jaky Solomon) to make a dress, her landlord to redecorate her apartment, and a pawnbroker to loan her money (at a usurious rate) to pay for it all. Her plan succeeds, Sonya and Manning marry, and she dreams that together they will right the world's social wrongs. "Their combined personalities would prove a titanic power that would show the world how the problems of races and classes, the rich and the poor, educated and uneducated, would be solved."

But the aloofness and superiority that once attracted her quickly becomes oppressive. He is her opposite in everything—abstract, indirect, and impersonal. She feels smothered in his social world and comes to hate the cold, indifferent tone he imposes on the settlement. Yezierska writes:

> Sonya and Manning, tricked into matrimony, were the oriental and the Anglo-Saxon trying to find a common language. The over-emotional Ghetto struggling for its air in the thin air of Puritan restraint. An East-Side savage forced suddenly into the strait-jacket of American civilization.

Finally, Sonya tells Manning what she thinks of him and his settlement and reveals her dealings with the usurer. He says their relationship is over but he will not divorce her. She flees, goes to work for a dressmaker, studies to be a designer, is rediscovered by Hollins, becomes his partner, receives a divorce from Manning, and marries Hollins.

A treatment adhering closely to the novel received low marks from a studio reader who noted that the mismatch idea

> is perhaps too subtle for the screen. The author gives an analysis of the unhappy married life of Manning and Sonya, and sets forth the impossibility of fusion between the Jew and the Gentile, and the patrician and the plebeian (and in a lesser degree the slav and the anglo-saxon).
>
> All the adverse criticism of the novel was directed against these chapters, and they really set out to prove too much, and end by proving nothing.

The reader recommended a revised treatment, developing "the pathos and charm of Hollins."[12]

Instead, the studio hired Sonya Levien to adapt it for the screen. She agreed, since the studio intended to shoot the film in New York. Levien's diary entry of December 26, 1924, notes Yezierska's name and telephone number, indicating they may have had some communication about the scenario. (There is no evidence that they maintained contact after that.)[13]

Levien changed the plot radically, making Manning a much more sympathetic and tolerant person, sharply reducing Hollins's part, and focusing the "problem" on Sonya's deviousness about the loan. When Manning indicts the usurer, the usurer entraps Sonya in a theft of the note and threatens to have her arrested if his indictment is pursued. Manning discovers the scheme, threatens the usurer with a blackmail charge, pays off the note, forgives Sonya, and the two live happily ever after.

The reviews were tepid, praising the director but criticizing the script. The *New York Times* (February 24, 1925) called it "an agreeable entertainment. With a little more concentration on the possibilities of the story it might have been less obvious and considerably strengthened." *Variety* (February 25) labeled it "a disappointment.…It has all the earmarks of something that has been hashed and rehashed as to story in order to get something out of it.…It is a mighty wishy-washy tale at its best." And the New York *Journal* found it "almost devoid of anything more than ordinary work."[14]

While writing that script, Levien, stimulated by the case of Leopold and Loeb (two young wealthy Jewish men who kidnapped and killed a young boy, Bobby Franks), composed a long, reflective article on her Jewishness and the current state of Jewish morality in the United States. "We were three Jews at a chance reunion," it began. Two had married out of the faith, all "had wandered from our fold by conscious choice," and yet we "agreed, without premeditation, intuitively and positively, that had young Leopold and Loeb been brought up in the orthodox faith, the crime would never have occurred." Reviewing her own training in *Talmud* and the *Shulhan Arukh*, which paralleled that of the training of an Orthodox Jew, Levien concluded that the Orthodox Jewish technique of using the fear of wrongdoing, of sin, was the best means of instilling virtue in the young. Among Jews in the United States today, she argues, only the Orthodox have maintained their spiritual ideals and morality, their passion for law and order.

> I would not choose the orthodox Jew for a bosom companion, but I respect him greatly—far more than the second generation type of American Jew, who thinks himself superior to his traditions....The Jew in this country has lost his religion too quickly, before he has found other ideals and customs to take the place of his old ones.[15]

Levien's sense of morality may have been heightened by these reflections, but her writing had always stressed fidelity and truth overcoming opportunism. As to her Jewishness, there is no evidence that she became more attentive to Jewish rituals and teachings or imposed an Orthodox sensibility on her children. She certainly did not feel an uncritical kinship with other Jews. The antagonism many Russian Jewish immigrants harbored toward their condescending German co-religionists stuck with her and, just prior to United States entry into World War II, she commented unfavorably on the superiority complexes of German Jews. She repeated a story told her by Arnold Schönberg about a meeting of exiled Jews in Belgrade endeavoring to form a self-protective organization. "One of the first speakers, a [German] woman, declared that the immediate thing to do was to exclude from the organization the Polish and Galician Jews, since they were inferior."[16]

Shortly after finishing *Salome*, Levien became a scenario

editor for Samuel Goldwyn Pictures. She attended Broadway plays, summarized their plots, and inquired about movie rights. Abraham Lehr wrote her, following the transfer of the department to Hollywood, "Your connection with us was an exceedingly happy experience for me and during the entire period of your engagement I knew you were earnestly and capably cooperating with us and loyally following up our interests." He also thanked her for "the careful manner in which you have kept records and files in the New York office."[17]

That job ended at the same time as Hovey's tenure as editor of *Hearst's International Magazine* (the renamed *Metropolitan*). They decided to move to Hollywood—she to write scenarios, he as a story editor for C. B. DeMille. When Clarence Day heard the news, he wrote her:

> Good Lord, Sonya! California again? Sold yourself into slavery like a Circassian dancer, to amuse languid audiences. What a queer life writers lead. They have to learn to give milk every day just like a cow—only some of them give pretty cheesy milk. Limburger cheese....What a life you have led, what a modern career you are having![18]

Carl did not hold the DeMille job long and failed to find another in the movie industry. S. N. Behrman, who knew the Hoveys well, wrote that Carl lost his job because of his reserve. The production people found him too intellectual. Sonya thought he read too much. "It's an opiate....It ruined Carl." He did some writing, including two scripts for Fox Film Corp. (*Orient Express* and *Three on a Honeymoon*, both 1934), and later worked for the Office of War Information, but he ceased to have a career. Behrman later wrote about "the somber aspect of Carl, the emanation of defeat." In general, his position in life, Behrman thought, "was awful." And yet, to Behrman's amazement, Hovey "was always humorous, always charming."[19] William Ludwig did not think Carl lived in limbo, did not see him as a frustrated man, but Tamara Hovey, in her autobiographical novel, *Among the Survivors,* depicts an angry, frustrated father, unable to complete any books, totally dependent on his wife's studio earnings.

Sonya, meanwhile, flourished. Several feature stories heralded her return. She told one interviewer:

> It was pleasantly surprising, and even startling to find how far the movies advanced during the year that I was away from active contact with them. When I came back to the work, they were accepting a rather different, and higher type of story, for filming.

Nevertheless, she still found Hollywood films unequal artistically to those produced in Europe, because the size of the American audience and the cost of the American film dictated "a lower common denominator of artistic appreciation." But she thought she saw new heights of achievement ahead for the American motion picture industry.[20]

In another piece, Levien spoke at length on the life of a career woman with children.

> A career and children are always conflicting, but one is a spur to the other. When you are out in the world, there is a companionship you can give your children that other mothers haven't. There's an enforced respect for your opinion because you are already in the battle that youngsters long for. That I think is the important factor between the working mother and the children.

Though her instincts pushed her to have six or seven children because "big families are great fun," and "it is good for children to grow up with brothers and sisters," she felt the economic system was entirely against it, especially in cases where women were working. Children, she continued, take a certain number of years away from a woman's career, and if she wanted more than one, she had to bear them in rapid sequence, while she was in her twenties.

> By the time a woman has reached her thirties, there has been such a struggle to get to a point of relative success that she can't meet with equilibrium the thought of beginning all over again on a new economic venture. Therefore, there's the tendency to postpone having another baby until you suddenly find your form of living has become established and to have one would be too uprooting.

She was, she admitted, dependent on servants. "Emergencies, like having servants leave unexpectedly, are the dread of a professional woman's life—her black moments. Therefore, we must arrange matters so as to allow the least possible chance for such happenings." Nevertheless, she did have her domestic side, and she resented the slurs cast on career women.

> I sacrifice every kind of plan that threatens to interfere with the routine of our home life and the physical welfare of our children....Just because I am not a good cook or fond of sewing and prefer going out and doing that for which I am infinitely better suited doesn't mean that I am indifferent to my house....The women that I know who do not work are restless wives who spend most of their time playing cards, sitting on the club piazzas and going to the matinee. I can't see that they are in their homes any more than I am....The childrens' training would be no different if I were home all the time, because I am a very poor teacher and would have them taught by experts.

She taught them what she knew: Russian nursery rhymes and a love for music.

Before examining Levien's career in Hollywood, several questions should be posed. Why did an intelligent, clear- and strong-minded, ambitious, skilled, educated, and accomplished woman devote the bulk of her professional writing career depicting women whose main attributes were spiritedness and pluck, who found satisfaction and happiness only in marriage? Why was there no evidence in her scripts, and little in her nonstudio life, of her once-radical political sensibility? Why, in sum, was she able to adapt herself so completely to the Hollywood studio system?

She wanted to succeed as a Hollywood screenwriter, and successful screenwriters mainly wrote to order, to meet the conventional demands of their conventional bosses, and maintained low political profiles to avoid antagonizing their politically conservative bosses. Carl Hovey's lack of steady employment saddled Sonya with the responsibility of supporting him, their two children, perhaps his two children from his first marriage, and a large household. In addition, the Hoveys preferred Hollywood's musical culture to its political salons.

Levien did make several efforts to maintain her independence as a writer. She continued to write stories for magazines and attempted to write plays. In her story, "Doubling in Love," Levien told the story of Cherry, a stand-in actress, trying to prove to William, a star, that "her own tender devotion" was worth more than the shallow glamour of Violet, William's co-star. Cherry was "humble and willing to wait" and clever enough to devise a stratagem to win William. Levien's one-act play, *By the Sword,* about an "unregenerate daughter," was performed by the Writers Club. The reviewer in the Los Angeles *Evening Herald* (June 30, 1927) commended the dialogue but thought the idea and characters required a three-act treatment. [22]

Levien also managed to avoid categorization as a writer of women's pictures. She was always considered an all-purpose writer, capable of handling most of the popular genres (westerns and gangster films excepted), and especially skilled at adaptation of material from other media.

During her first four years back in Hollywood, she gravitated from studio to studio, at first using the name Sonya

Hovey. In her first stint at Warner Bros. (January-June 1926), she began to write farcical comedy, but only her fourth script for that studio, *Footloose Widows,* represents a new dimension for her. In it, Levien graduates from melodrama with comedic elements to screwball-type comedy: juxtaposition of the poor and wealthy, mistaken identities, gold digging, con games, and so on. She wrote a circus potboiler for Banner Productions, *Christine of the Big Tops,* and a much more sophisticated screwball comedy, *The Princess from Hoboken,* for Tiffany Productions.

Cecil B. DeMille then hired her to write for his studios, Metropolitan Pictures and Pathé (August 1926-June 1928). Clarence Day wrote to her, in November 1927: "You sound to me as though you were in a treadmill. To provide for one's old age and children uses up all one's steam."[23] It certainly strained her inventiveness as she went from genre to genre.

In *The Heart Thief,* she adapted a convoluted romance set in Hungary. *A Harp in Hock,* her best screenplay to date, returned her to the world of the Lower East Side, where a lonely pawnshop owner adopts an orphaned boy. Their poignant and complicated relationship, however, is diluted by the necessary romantic side plot. She regressed badly in *A Ship Comes In,* originally titled "His Country." There she demonstrated how readily she could shed her radical past and adopt a sappy nationalism. Using a distorted version of the Sacco and Vanzetti case, Levien depicted anarchists in an unfair and preposterous manner and copiously slathered on love of country. Just off the ship from Hungary, Peter Plecznick and his family go to a coffee shop to meet neighbors from the old country. While they are talking, anarchists are meeting in the basement.

> This scene is to be based on the picture by John Collier[24] except that instead of the man holding up a bomb, there will be Sokol standing up and delivering a fiery anarchistic speech.... Alex Sokol is a big, strong man with bushy hair, and

blustering argumentative manner....On one side of Sokol sits Gregor—short, stock-headed and brutal. On the other side of Sokol sits Semyon—a pale, tense, fanatical type.

Overhearing Peter praising the United States, Sokol "interrupts Peter rudely, and declares argumentatively: 'All governments are alike—favoring the rich, oppressing the poor!'" Peter argues with him.

Five years later, with the United States at war, Peter awaits his naturalization test while Judge Gresham sentences Gregor to ten years at hard labor and tells the convicted man, "You foreign-born agitators, who use your American citizenship to mask acts of treachery, are the most dangerous and despicable of all enemies." The other members of the group, Sokol, Semyon, "a stolid woman or two and four men of varied fanatical types," decide to assassinate the judge with a bomb. The bomb is placed in a cake Peter's wife baked for the judge. It kills the judge's secretary and gravely wounds the judge. Peter is tried and convicted for the crime. But when Sokol hears of the death of Peter's son in combat, he goes mad with remorse and confesses. Peter, instead of expressing anger at the miscarriage of justice, exclaims, "I knew Uncle Sam would set me free!"[25]

Sonya's last assignment, a newspaper-story treatment, was budgeted much lower than the other three movies on which she had worked, and the studio did not assign her to write the scenario. In search of another job and hyperconscious of appearing as a female writer rather than a writer who happened to be female, Sonya wrote the man who had interviewed her at Fox Film Corp.:

> I am sorry I was such a dumb dora when I saw you yesterday afternoon. It isn't that I am over-modest, but I have such a horror of the female scenarist who pierces you with a fanatical eye and tells you, foaming at the mouth, what a brilliant 100 per center she is, that I usually act perversely when it comes to selling myself. And since I was the fifth female in line

within a period of half an hour, I was conscious that you had your fill of the poisonous species.

I kicked myself afterwards because I never mentioned to you the one thing nearest my heart as a screen writer—and that is to tell my story on the screen in its dominant mood—and keep to it throughout, clothing the business and the characterization with the glamour of that mood. It is that thing which gives a screen story a chance to have a "distinctive style"—in the same manner that every bit of distinctive literature has its style.

...I hope that some day, when I am not so aware of asking for work, I shall get a chance to talk to you about it.[26]

She also sent a list of her screen credits and the magazines that published her stories to agent Myron Selznick.[27]

In the autumn, she signed with Columbia Pictures and wrote her two best scenarios to date, both directed by Frank Capra. *The Power of the Press* is a conventional newspaper story, but the pace is excellent. There is no dawdling over any of the elements. The second, *The Younger Generation,* based on a story by Fannie Hurst, is a compelling tale of immigrant and family identity. Morris Goldfish overcomes his parents' poverty, achieves wealth and social acceptance, and tries to bury his past. Ashamed of every aspect of his origins, especially his parents' customs, he alienates sister, parents, and fiancée. Here again, the pace is good and the situations are believably and dramatically rendered. The ending, with Morris left alone and lonely, is perfectly bleak.[28] Capra's and Columbia's first talkie, *The Younger Generation* combined largely silent exterior scenes with synchronized sound dialogues. In his autobiography, Capra described it as a movie "about the super-Jew who denied his parents," and Levien as "the out-going scriptwriter with the infectious laugh."[29] The reviews were not particularly complimentary.

Her last two assignments for Columbia were unremarkable. *Trial Marriage* was a trite, overly complicated boy-meets-loses-regains-girl story, and *The Quitter,* about a doctor who fails to save his mother's life but seventy alienated minutes later saves the life of a stranger under impossible conditions, did not earn her a credit. She and the studio parted company in March 1929.

Meanwhile, she had been elected to the board of the Writers Club, a sort of gentleman's-gentlewoman's organization of screen writers. Though it was affiliated with the Authors' League of America, it was not a union and made no effort at collective bargaining. Few writers in Hollywood in those days considered themselves "workers" and hence disdained the concept of a labor union. Many simply trusted in the *noblesse oblige* or paternalism of the heads of studios or production. Invariably, most were disappointed. For example, Lenore Coffee had ultimate faith in Irving Thalberg, to the point of not even using an agent to negotiate her contracts. In 1931, she chose M-G-M over Goldwyn when both offered her $1,000. Thalberg then slashed her salary in half without warning her and refused, without telling her, dozens of offers from other studios to borrow her services at the higher rate. When that contract expired, she hired an agent.[30]

In May 1929, Fox Film Corp. offered Levien the opportunity she thought she had mishandled a year earlier, signing her to a contract that would be renewed regularly until 1939.

Chapter 5

At Fox and Twentieth Century-Fox

William Fox had moved from the garment industry to the exhibition end of the motion picture industry in 1904, founded a studio and national distributing system in 1912, merged all three components into the Fox Film Corp. in 1915, and opened his first Hollywood studio in 1917. For the first year or so, the Fox Film Corp. tackled challenging social themes such as prison reform, until Fox decided those films were too costly and switched to cheaper pictures with more profitable subjects.[1] When he began to lose ground to Paramount and Loew's in the late 1920s, he sent his vice president and general manager, Winfield Sheehan, to build and supervise a new studio in West Los Angeles.

Sheehan had been a newspaper reporter and secretary to both the New York City fire and police commissioners and had organized the first Fox studio in Hollywood and the domestic and foreign distribution branches. A short, paunchy Irishman, Sheehan was "a complex character: affable, sentimental, suspicious, cynical, ruthless, and a squat dynamo of energy. His baby-blue eyes popped out from a florid face that was seldom relaxed. [He] loved to play God."[2] He abandoned the individual star method and concentrated on acquiring good stories and carefully fitting starring and supporting players to their story characters. While Sheehan revamped production, Fox borrowed heavily from Wall

Street to purchase more theaters and, in a few years, the studio had regained parity with Paramount.[3]

Levien went to work for Fox during this upswing. Her first yearly contract called for her to receive $500 per week for the first six months and $600 per week for the second, with a one-year renewal option at $750. But the legal department rejected her request for a clause giving her screen credit and publicity for every script on which she worked and permission to advertise her work in the trade papers at her own expense.[4]

Levien joined a prominent group of female screenwriters at Fox—Zoë Akins, Clare Kummer, Marion Orth, and Elinor Glyn. She immediately became one of Sheehan's top writers, assigned to work with the studio's biggest stars and most important directors. She wrote four screenplays for Charles Farrell and Janet Gaynor, two for Janet Gaynor, and five for Will Rogers. Frank Borzage directed six of her scenarios, Allan Dwan three, and John Ford three. She only worked on one script for the studio's biggest star, Shirley Temple—an uncredited addition to *Curly Top* (a remake of the *Daddy Long Legs* script she had written for Gaynor). Between 1929 and the arrival of Darryl F. Zanuck in mid-1935, Levien worked on an average of six screenplays a year, averaging five credits.

S. N. Behrman, who met her in 1929 and collaborated with her on eight screenplays during the 1930s, wrote:

> She was very attractive with lustrous black hair and big blue eyes....She was warm, overflowing with vitality, an instant darling. She spoke an engaging pidgin English; she was constantly saying: 'That's exactly!' You never knew quite about what.

Sensitive about her English and the expressions she used, Sonya was mimicked and teased by her husband and Behrman. "I think there were times when we overdid it," Behrman wrote later. Because she was an exceedingly generous and popular woman who "took on everyone who came her way," Behrman found it impossible to get any work done in Sonya's studio office. It seemed to him as though every writer with whom she had ever worked came to her for help.[5]

Levien described herself in a studio "Color Biography" as a person who dislikes shopping and talking on the telephone but loves singing, playing the piano, reading (mainly biographies), and dogs. Though fond of pretty clothes, she hates to dress up and usually wears sports clothes. Possessing all the Russian instincts of impracticability, she is seldom on time for anything and frequently misses trains. Though she quarrels with herself, she avoids arguing with friends, preferring to allow them to have their own way. She thinks of herself as ambitious but restless. In 1932, a studio publicist described Levien as the possessor of a wonderful smile, dark brown hair, blue eyes and a fresh peachblow complexion—a Russian Jewess who looks more like a Russian colleen.[6]

Though she appeared agreeable, Sonya's lengthy survival in the movie industry depended much more on a perdurable toughness and ambition she only occasionally displayed. For example, at the end of her first year at the studio, shortly after her contract was renewed, she wrote a strongly worded memo to William Crawford of the legal department:

> In this morning's paper, in a huge announcement of Will Rogers' opening [*So This is London*], everybody connected with the picture is given credit....Although I rewrote the second half of the story completely, wrote a new beginning and was responsible, with Mr. Rogers himself, for all of the dialogue, my name is not mentioned. This is a repetition of what happened in the case of *They Had to See Paris*. ...In the case of the McCormack picture [*Song O' My Heart*]...the same thing happened....It seems to be a settled policy to omit my name from all the advertising and publicity concerning the pictures on which I work for the company. I have it in my contract that I am to get credit for what I write. I regard this

persistent ignoring of my work and worth to a picture as a breach of contract and a personal insult.[7]

Though Sonya's salary and the quality of her credits continued to increase, she noted, in an article on screenwriting for an anthology entitled *Careers for Women*:

> the motion-picture business is notoriously a hard profession. Writers—good ones—are extremely sensitive persons. A screenwriter finds himself part of a ponderous moving machine, working in conditions which make it fatal to think of one's personal feelings. The reward for stoicism, for courage, for tremendous persistence under difficulties and under pressure, comes when the picture is finished and is a success. If it turns out to be good, you have the excitement of winning a battle—and the money in your pocket—or, if it turns out badly, you still have the money. There is nothing in the screenwriting profession for a woman who wants a quiet, peaceful life or for a writer who is ambitious for literary fame.[8]

Levien had two particular strengths as a screenwriter. She could write filmable scripts quickly and without fuss, adapting virtually any type of property. She thought that adaptation was her greatest skill, a carryover from her days as a fiction editor.

> I treated a book with respect and concentrated on getting the author's every thought over to the screen....I struggle to retain that spark of life which has made that piece of literature survive, and because of which the picture people have bought it.[9]

She developed a reputation for her ability to reconstruct sick scripts, but she never became known for the quality of her dialogue. In fact, on her first dozen scripts for Fox (all talkies), she shared the credits with another writer—she designated for continuity, he for dialogue.

Her second strength consisted of a perfect intermediary's disposition. Guy Bolton, her co-writer on *Delicious,* said about her, "Sonya is a liaison officer between good taste and the picture business." And she said about herself, "my own life is a continual strain of dealing with charming and disarming racketeers."[10] She seemed to have virtually no ego investment in story integrity, plot rendering, characterization, or fidelity to the source; she never complained about art being sacrificed to commerce. She did not, that is, writhe privately or publicly in the snares of the studio writing process.

She began her Fox career with a detective thriller, *Behind that Curtain,* the third Charlie Chan story to be filmed in Hollywood. The studio had paid Earl Der Biggers $5,000 for the rights, and Sheehan described it as the "biggest selling sensational mystery serial story ever published in *Saturday Evening Post.*"[11] Sonya altered the plot substance and reduced Chan's role.

Her second assignment began a long-term collaboration with Frank Borzage, Janet Gaynor, and Charles Farrell. Borzage seemed to prefer female writers and stories written by women. Frances Marion, for example, wrote four movies he directed between 1923-26. But no one who writes about Borzage's career mentions these writers.[12] Georges Sadoul, for example, wrote, "His lovers are rarely isolated from their environment, but are carefully depicted as part of their times."[13] When *Lucky Star,* Levien and Borzage's first collaboration, was restored and shown at Telluride and UCLA (1991), it was labeled "Frank Borzage's *Lucky Star.*"

Notes in the *Lucky Star* script indicate that Levien either consulted with Borzage as she wrote or revised the material after he had read and commented on it. For example, some seventy scenes were replaced by a series of transitional dissolves "as discussed with Mr. Borzage," and a subplot involving another war veteran was eliminated—"Mr. Borzage has definitely decided to leave Pop Fry out."[14] The finished product featured Janet Gaynor and Charles Farrell—he as a paraplegic war veteran, she as a plucky gamine. She had always loved him; he realizes his love for her when she washes her face, combs her hair, puts on a new dress, and becomes the object of an unscrupulous suitor. To find the happiness they seek, they merely have to overcome her bullying mother, the sexually abusive suitor, and Farrell's paraplegia. The reviews were poor.

Their next project, *They Had to See Paris,* Will Rogers' first talkie, received positive reviews. It used a conventional format to spotlight Rogers' appeal—Oklahoman strikes oil; family becomes snooty; family discovers, with the aid of the homespun philosophy of the husband/father, that home and old rural values are the best. Rogers adored Levien and, in his newspaper column, termed her *"the best female scenario writer."*[15]

Borzage and Levien's third movie, *Song O' My Heart,* was their best. One of Borzage's biographers calls it "the main transition film" between his silent and sound work and credits him with integrating the music and lyrics to add dimension to the plot.[16] Basically following the lines of world-famous tenor John McCormack's life, Levien's script situated him in his small Irish village next to the woman he has always loved and her children. When she dies, he arranges their future lives. A romantic subplot was added to provide the conflict that did not exist in the singer's life. The reviewers particularly complimented the writing. "The story is charming and sensitive," wrote the *New York Times* reviewer. "The comedy is gentle and natural" (March 12, 1930). "It is spiced with more interwoven legitimate comedy," wrote *Variety,* "than any talker to date" (March 19).

Their other three projects failed to achieve the quality of *Song,* though *Liliom* is notable for uniting Levien with S. N. Behrman. One of a number of young playwrights enticed to early sound-era Hollywood, Behrman finally acceded after two of his plays failed and Winfield Sheehan offered him

$1,250 a week to help adapt Ferenc Molnar's play *Liliom*. Behrman worked steadily in Hollywood for the next ten years, riding the rails between there and Broadway. As he sat on the *Super Chief* on this first trip, he worried about a scenario that killed the hero halfway through, sent him to heaven, and then arranged for him to revisit those he had left behind. He had, he wrote, "no natural taste or liking for fantasy.... Perhaps Sonya Levien with all her experience would know what to do about heaven. I began to be grateful to her before I met her."

Sonya was delighted to be working with Behrman, delighted they would be writing for Borzage, whom she adored, and evidenced little concern for Behrman's heaven problem. Behrman later wrote, "It's fun working with Sonya....[S]he makes me laugh—and if you don't laugh in the picture business, you cry." Scriptwriting was too much trouble, he concluded, unless he worked with her.[17]

Though the play had been a great success, it is difficult to fathom why. The hero, Liliom, is a brute, and his return-to-earth scenes are hard to swallow. Because of the play's success, the screenwriters could do little with either. All they could do was give him some charm and saving graces, while making the transitions from heaven to earth flow as smoothly as possible. Levien wrote the adaptation and continuity, Behrman the dialogue. The final script completed, they met with Sheehan's assistant, Sol Wurtzel, who began the script conference by saying, "I don't like a picture where the hero dies in the middle! Especially if he's Charlie Farrell." Behrman, Borzage, and the scene designer tried to convince Wurtzel that his concern was misplaced, but he remained unmoved. "All that heaven stuff don't mean a thing to me. I don't know what it's all about.... What's wonderful about it? It shows—he was a punk on earth and he's a punk in heaven. What benefit did he get from dying?"[18] Wurtzel's instinct proved accurate. *Liliom* received mixed reviews and was not a major success.

Behrman and Levien collaborated on three of her next six assignments, none of them memorable, though *Lightnin'*, for Will Rogers, received the expected good reviews and box office. Levien also received her first solo credit, for *Daddy Long Legs*, though Behrman made some revisions and worked on the dialogue of this hoary Hollywood formula: older, wealthy man assists younger, poorer beauty. Love blossoms, misunderstandings abound, they transcend, they wed. A few pictures later, in *The Brat*, Levien and Behrman added a twist to the formula, allowing the younger wastrel brother to end up with the adopted gamine. Levien also inserted one of her first risqué scenes and sly commentary on it. In a scene where the Brat is dancing, Levien appends a note to director John Ford: "Her skirt jerks up and there is a degree of posterior exposure that would fill Raoul Walsh with envy!"[19] (Walsh was notorious for sneaking risqué scenes and dialogue past the studio censors.) In fact, according to Ludwig, Levien's reputation for sweetness and purity made her the perfect vehicle for explaining to studio censors the innocent intent of borderline salacious material.

During her second year at Fox, Levien was assigned a labor of love—a script written to accommodate a grab bag of George Gershwin tunes. Levien and Guy Bolton contrived their script to fit the music, Ira Gershwin wrote lyrics to match the script, and George wrote an orchestral rhapsody depicting the hustle and bustle of Manhattan specifically for the movie. George wrote to her, during the filming:

> I cannot tell you how badly I feel because I am not able to come out to help on our picture. I am sort of depending on it to be not only a big hit, but a very worthy effort....I would appreciate it so much if you would interest yourself in the musical end of it to the extent of letting me know how our end of it is progressing.[20]

Delicious starred Janet Gaynor (as a brave, practical, but poor Scottish immigrant) and Charles Farrell (as a wealthy, but simple horse breeder). It opened widely on Christmas 1931 and received pallid reviews. The reviewer for the *New York Times* called the story "a conventional piece of sentimentality with dialogue that is scarcely inspired" (December 26, 1931). *Variety* termed it "a technically mediocre talker" (December 29).

However, Levien and the Gershwins formed a lasting friendship (fourteen years later, Levien would write a treatment for a Warner Bros. biography of George Gershwin, *Rhapsody in Blue*). The Hoveys also came to know Leopold Stokowski and Arnold Schönberg and regularly hosted a musically based salon. The Hovey house was filled with musical instruments, including two pianos, because Oscar Levant and Harpo Marx liked to play duets. At one gathering in 1938, an unused Gershwin song from *Shall We Dance*—"Hi-Ho! At Last!"—was home recorded, with Harold Arlen playing the piano and Ira Gershwin singing.[21]

Three of Levien's next four scripts were intended for Gaynor, although Gaynor only starred in two of them. About *Tess of the Storm Country*, her last with Behrman at Fox, Levien wrote a friend who had confessed he had acted most unloyally by not seeing it when it played in his area: "The most loyal thing you could have done was *not* see [it]."[22]

At the end of 1931, Fox underwent its second executive upheaval within a 24-month period. In April 1930, bankers forced William Fox to resign from the company he had founded. Sheehan, who had sided against Fox (and sued him), remained in full control of the studio. But in December 1931, with a huge loss pending ($2.9 million), a headline in *The Hollywood Reporter* proclaimed a mass firing of executives, salary cuts, and a production takeover by New Yorkers. On December 16, Sheehan was said to be ill with a nervous condition. One month later, the trade daily reported another major housecleaning on the lot, a "slaughter," and Sheehan's three-month leave of absence to recover from a nervous breakdown.

During his absence, the production heads decided to institute a cycle of big, expensive movies. They began by paying $100,000 for the rights to Noël Coward's British nationalist play, *Cavalcade*. Sol Wurtzel sent Borzage, Levien, and Behrman to London to see the play. Despite its very British slice of history (Boer War to 1932), deeply died patriotism, and upstairs/downstairs interactions, all three were impressed. They anticipated no difficulty in making it appealing to American viewers.[23]

Levien saw in the play several universal themes: the suffering and defeat that accompanies victory in war and the tragedy of mothers whose sons die in battle. "In transforming the story to the screen I felt that the most important contribution I could make was to have the good taste not to spoil it." But Sheehan, on his return, did not approve the Levien/Behrman adaptation and imported British playwright Reginald Berkeley to start from the beginning. When he finished the script, Levien was assigned to revise it and add dialogue.

Fox spent $1.3 million on the movie, a huge expenditure, considering the straitened economy, the unpopularity of war movies, and the unrelenting Britishness of the product. When it was completed, Levien recalled:

> The New York bankers came out to see the finished picture. It was shown in Mr. Sheehan's private projection room to about seventy people—almost all of them men. This was no social occasion but a cold appraisal by hard-headed business men and picture professionals. There were no laughs, no tears, no applause. And when the lights went up again it was on a wake. The unanimous opinion was that the picture was too British, and wouldn't make a penny in America. Why the heck didn't the writer turn it into an American story?

Sheehan released it to glowing reviews, receipts of over $5

million, and an Academy Award for best picture (1932-33). Noël Coward wired Levien, "I knew last spring that you understood and appreciated 'Cavalcade'; and I have seen the splendid proof of it this afternoon."[24]

Sheehan then assigned Levien to another big-budget picture, intended for Will Rogers and Janet Gaynor, adapting Phil Stong's best-selling novel, *State Fair,* a congenial, simply written morality play about the Frake family's week at the fair. Ostensibly it is about winning prizes for best hog and best pickles, but it is really about the sexual awakening and maturation of the two Frake teenagers. The book's author, Phil Stong, and Julian Josephson had been signed to adapt it. But, according to Levien, Stong had heard too much about "love, sex, and glamour," so he dumped his own story about the Frake family's visit to the state fair "and came up with something that looked more like an original."

Sheehan and director Henry King did not like the departure from the novel. A depressed Stong told Levien that screenwriting was not the profession for him and that *State Fair* was not, after all, "a good book. If only I could write it all over again!"[25] Paul Green then wrote a new screenplay, providing a sounder dramatic structure, but it still failed to satisfy the producer and director. Levien, next up, went back to the novel and wrote a screenplay that stayed faithful to the book's episodic qualities and dialogue. When the studio announced that Green's name would precede hers on the screen credit, she strenuously objected, and the story department backed her claim to precedence. The finished product received terrific reviews and returned several million dollars in profits to the studio, which would remake the movie twice as a musical, in 1945 and 1962. Levien and Green were nominated for the Academy Award for best adaptation.

At the end of 1932, Sonya's old friend Jesse Lasky came to Fox with a contract to produce eight movies, of which Levien wrote five, including the last pairing of Gaynor and Farrell (*Change of Heart*). At this stage, she was being paid $1,000 a week, and the studio had agreed to allow her to advertise her work in the trades. The studio had inserted her picture and credits in the midst of a 25-page ad celebrating the studio, and she, three months later, paid for her own ad, mentioning *State Fair*, *Cavalcade*, and her first project for Lasky, *The Warrior's Husband*.[26]

The last was a comedy of reversed sexual stereotypes adapted from a play very loosely based on *Lysistrata*. The opening title card establishes the premise:

> Back in 800 B.C.—believe it or not—the land of Pontius was ruled by Amazons. These strapping women were the warriors and providers. They had all the rights—and pretty good lefts—and believed that man's place was in the home.

At first, the gender convention reversals were amusing and witty, especially the demands of the men to be allowed to do what women do, including dressing like a warrior. But the film soon descended into a typical screwball romance, with women being softened and their enterprises compromised by their attraction to conniving men, and the viewer was left with a series of caustic commentaries on the dangers of women's liberation. The ending title card read:

> In 1933 A.D.—believe it or not—nothing has changed. Women are still fighters, and believe that man's place is in the home.[27]

The studio's reader pointed out that this script could raise problems with the Code office if it was not carefully handled in filming. "The most obvious danger is the possibility of portraying the women warriors in a manner which is perfectly acceptable for men, but which would be resented when played by women, and the other, the possibility of characterizing the men as effeminate to the point of resentment."[28] Filmed as a heavy-handed burlesque rather than a light satire, the movie, without any major stars, received middling reviews.

The Great Depression hit the movie industry hard in 1932 and 1933. The trade papers reported a $100 million loss for 1932, with only Loew's and Columbia showing a profit. Paramount and RKO were in receivership, and overhead cuts were forecast for every studio. In February 1933, *The Hollywood Reporter* noted that at Fox 250 employees had been fired and everyone else's salary had been cut 20 percent. Levien "volunteered" to lower her weekly take to $900. But more sacrifices were deemed necessary. In early March, a joint meeting of the producers association and the Board of Governors of the Academy of Motion Picture Arts and Sciences announced that unless those studio employees earning more than $50 per week agreed to a 50 percent salary cut for eight weeks, the studios would close for eight weeks. Using President Franklin D. Roosevelt's declaration of a national bank holiday as the occasion, studio heads herded all the writers, directors, actors, cameramen, etc., into the studio commissaries, shed copious tears, and announced the cut. The employees were asked to sign a "waiver" designed by an industry emergency committee. Levien agreed to waive 50 percent of her original salary, $1,000, for the period March 6-April 30. At the same time, she was offered a renewed contract for $1,000 per week.[29]

However, a small group of writers, infuriated by the lack of protection the pay cut demonstrated, reorganized the heretofore ineffectual Screen Writers Guild to bargain for a standard contract protecting all writers from arbitrary decisions on wages, credits, layoffs, etc. By April it had enrolled 300 writers; within a year, it would have over 600. To gain leverage, Guild leaders asked all writers due for contract renewal to postpone signing new contracts until June 1, while a standard Code of Working Rules was drawn up. Levien was placed in a quandary. She did not want to risk losing the renewal, but she did not want "to be forced to violate her moral understanding" with the Guild. She asked the studio either to hold the contract in abeyance or to allow her to sign it in secret, and then, on June 1, tear it up and allow her to sign an identical contract. The legal department chose the latter procedure.[30]

In August 1935, the owners of Twentieth Century Pictures, Joseph Schenck and Darryl F. Zanuck, bought controlling interest in the Fox company and created the Twentieth Century-Fox Film Corp. Sheehan, unwilling to assume a subordinate position in production decisions, sold his interest in the studio. Zanuck, who had once been a screenwriter, assumed control over production. Writers who worked for him referred to him as "a writers' producer." Once he had approved a script, no one, not a producer or director or star, could alter it. According to screenwriter Philip Dunne, "the script was the star."[31] And yet, Zanuck had little confidence in most writers. In fact, he believed he was the greatest script editor alive. Virtually no screenplay at Twentieth emerged intact from Zanuck's marathon script conferences. Shortly after they ended, a lengthy typed transcript of his remarks appeared on the writers' desks. "He was not afraid," recalled screenwriter Sheridan Gibney, "of making changes."[32]

Many of the writers, however, felt constrained by the narrowness of the story material Zanuck assigned them and the limited range of the studio's main contract players. In fact, Zanuck produced so many costume epics in his first years that the studio became known as "Sixteenth Century-Fox." The characteristic Zanuck movie of that period featured a romanticized perspective on American history, a pageant of struggle and brawling smoothed at the end by the love of a good woman, mother, or wife.[33] In fairness to Zanuck, it should be noted that he had taken over a studio whose main adult star, Will Rogers, would die the following month, and whose main child star, Shirley Temple, was growing into a less-appealing adult. Janet Gaynor's star was dimming rapidly and the new generation—Alice Faye, Sonja Henie, Don

Ameche, and Tyrone Power—failed to match the glitter at M-G-M or Paramount or the toughness at Warner Bros.

Zanuck began his tenure by calling in and reading every script, rejecting twelve, and canceling six movies that were already in production. This included Levien's *The Captive Bride*, a romantic comedy involving a charming Italian aristocrat (a "liberal") who comes to the United States incognito to purchase oil and becomes enmeshed with the social-climbing daughter of the oil producer. At a time when a significant number of writers were mobilizing against fascism, Levien had written a script that contained no critical remarks about Benito Mussolini or Fascist Italy.

Zanuck installed a new production system: one supervising producer per movie, with Zanuck overseeing every production. Every script now came under Zanuck's close scrutiny, and every screenwriter faced long story conferences.

> One hard-backed chair was placed dead center in front of Zanuck's desk. The rest of the chairs were lined against the wall. The hard chair was the hot chair and everyone was afraid to sit there....Zanuck sat whom he wanted in the hot chair, and usually it was the Writer, or as he was more often known, to distinguish him from those who replaced him, "The Present Writer."[34]

Levien left behind no comments on Zanuck. She had worked with him at Warners during the 1920s on *Footloose Widows* and worked under him for four years at Twentieth. There he cut her workload enormously (she averaged three assignments a year for him), paid her $1,600 a week (making her one of the industry's highest-paid writers), and put her to work on some of his biggest movies.

The subject of Levien's first major picture under the new regime came directly from newspaper headlines: the tremendous publicity surrounding the birth of the Dionne quintuplets. The media hubbub had begun when the attending physician, Dr. Allan Dafoe, made a public plea for an incubator. The Chicago *American* sent one, along with reporter Charles E. Blake, whose stories created a major tourist attraction. Over 1 million tourists traveled to Callander, Ontario, to view the quints at play through a one-way window.

Zanuck bought Blake's story outline for $5,000 and outbid two other studios for the exclusive rights to film the quints. Blake came to Hollywood and was teamed with Levien to write a script for Will Rogers. Rogers had frequently mentioned that he wanted to play a country doctor and had once asked Levien to write such a role for him. In fact, Levien had co-written a plot outline entitled *The Country Doctor* for the studio in November 1930, but the outline was not approved for scripting.[35]

In any event, Blake and Levien began work with a file folder of newspaper clippings and no story hook. Tragically, Will Rogers's death in an airplane crash provided Levien with her inspiration. "I felt the world had suddenly dropped away," Levien wrote later. "I was so moved by [his] death that the idea came to me to tell [the Dionne] story from the point of view of a simple country doctor trying to cope with this amazing thing." It would be her memorial to Rogers.[36]

Using the actual doctor, Allan Roy Dafoe, as her model for Dr. John Luke, Sonya also added a faithful nurse (obviously in love with the doctor), a sympathetic sheriff, and a conflicted love story between two younger people. At the first script conference, Zanuck commanded the writers to build up the love story and parallel it with the doctor's difficulties, to give the story the strength it presently lacks. Zanuck also wanted more modern dialogue and more believable love scenes. Nunnally Johnson, a writer-producer at Fox, congratulated Sonya on the dramatic construction. It "is a superb job. To me you have captured completely the picture of Dafoe that we wanted to present. I can scarcely imagine it being done better."[37] Though Sonya received sole screenplay credit, Blake wrote that he tremendously enjoyed the opportunity of working with her.

The story was filmed on location in Callander, and Levien went with the crew. She became friendly with Dr. Dafoe and enchanted with the quints. A studio publicity release quoted her as saying:

> I am not a sentimental woman. I have two children of my own. I've been willing to turn them over to a competent nurse and carry on a career of my own. Yet when I watched these five little girls dressed, one by one, I wanted to handle them, to snuggle them. I wanted to put them all in a giant basket and take them home.[38]

After the picture had opened, Levien wrote to Dafoe:

> The most satisfying thing I have to report is the great success of our "Country Doctor." I hope with all my heart that you have seen it and *like it*. In fact, I am so anxious on that point that I would appreciate hearing from you. I saw it with several audiences. They loved it. In all my twelve years of scenario writing—and I have written some of the finest pictures in the industry—I have never heard such enthusiasm on the part of audiences.

Dafoe responded that he liked the movie. "It was good fiction, and full of human interests."[39]

With Jean Hersholt as the doctor, the movie received very good reviews and brought in $1.4 million in domestic rentals, second on the Fox list that year. Trying to capitalize on the acclaim that greeted Hersholt's work and the continued fame of the quints, Zanuck immediately assigned Levien to write a sequel. Though he approved the general continuity of that script, he criticized the dialogue and the characterizations. He assigned Sam Hellman and Gladys Lehman to do a complete rewrite but criticized their first draft for its lack of conflict, excitement, and surprise.[40] *Reunion* received the mediocre reviews it deserved, but Zanuck persisted with still another sequel, *Five of a Kind* (1938), without Levien's input.

Meanwhile, a virtual civil war had broken out between the studio heads and the Screen Writers Guild, precipitating a schism in the ranks of the writers. Unhappy with the antagonism between the guild and the studio bosses and the radical political bent of some of the guild leaders, a conservative group of writers calling themselves the "Liberal Group" tried to assume control in early 1934. They failed, but two years later, when the guild announced that it intended to amalgamate with the Authors' League, Dramatists Guild, Newspaper Guild, and Radio Writers Guild, the bosses went on the offensive, led by Irving Thalberg and Darryl F. Zanuck. Zanuck announced that amalgamation "promises the screenwriters that eventually they will be able to control the screen destinies of the stories they work on. I can imagine nothing that would kill this business any quicker."[41] He coupled that with a press release sent to all the Fox writers with a covering note, "for the purpose of emphasizing...how seriously the producing corporations believe the industry will be adversely affected by the activities of the present Guild leadership."[42]

Fueled by Thalberg, the conservative screenwriters, mainly at M-G-M, announced the formation of a new guild, the Screen Playwrights, Inc., and that same day the production companies announced their willingness to bargain with it. The Screen Writers Guild hemorrhaged members, including, it was alleged, 28 of the 43 under contract at Twentieth. The Playwrights, nothing more than a sweetheart union, never enrolled more than 100 writers, but Screen Writers Guild membership dipped very low, as most writers chose to remain unaffiliated until the contest was decided.

In 1937, taking advantage of the newly created National Labor Relations Board, the Screen Writers Guild regrouped. According to its figures, guild membership far exceeded Playwright membership at every studio, even M-G-M. At

Twentieth, it was alleged, there were 5 Playwright members, 31 guild members, and 21 nonaffiliates. At the certification election held in June 1938, the Screen Writers Guild swamped the Screen Playwrights, 271-57. At Twentieth, 38 voted for the Guild, 5 for the Playwrights.[43]

Levien had spoken against amalgamation at Screen Writers Guild meetings and would serve on the Screen Playwrights board. According to William Ludwig, her main collaborator in the last decade of her career:

> She was the least political person I ever met. She joined both the SP and the SWG, but she wasn't active in either. She was completely work-dominated and not political on industry matters. She had dear and old friends in every echelon, including the extreme left. When the SP set up shop, it was done by a bunch of old boys at Metro, her friends, the Thalberg-echelon group. It seemed like a good career-move to join, but she had no philosophical position.[44]

She was, he told me, an observer rather than a participant.

During that extraordinarily active political period in Hollywood history (1934-48), Levien maintained a very low profile. In her only overt political act, she hosted a huge cocktail and tea party welcoming to Hollywood her old friend, Frances Perkins, now Secretary of Labor in Franklin Roosevelt's New Deal administration. The February 1940 event featured a veritable who's who of Hollywood movie, arts, and political figures. In return, Perkins invited Levien to come to Washington to meet Eleanor Roosevelt.

Within the confines of Twentieth's story department, however, Levien wrote a script favorably presenting the rebellion led by Generalissimo Francisco Franco (supported by Fascist Italy and Nazi Germany) against the democratically elected government of Spain (supported by the U.S.S.R.). The cause of the government was hugely popular among Hollywood liberals and Communists. Conservatives and Catholics supported the rebels. Studio bosses, for their part, had no side, but all of them saw the cinematic possibilities of a movie about the civil war. Every studio launched at least one project with Spain as a background, but only a few uniformly bad movies resulted. Among those not produced was an original story by Sonya Levien, *The Siege of Alcazar*, based on the rebel defense of a citadel in Toledo.

The idea for the movie came from a series of articles, "70 Days in Hell," written by H. R. Knickerbocker, a syndicated reporter for the New York *Evening Journal*. To secure rights to the preferred title, *The Siege of the Alcazar*, which was not copyrighted, the studio bought his articles and war logs and made arrangements to have them published under that title. According to Louella O. Parsons, Zanuck was following "the Spanish War with the zest of a schoolboy reading Nick Carter novels." He had, she continued, also purchased the rights to a London play, Walter Hackett's *The Fugitives*, concerning the revolution in Barcelona.[46]

The opening portion of Levien's story simply describes the horrors of civil war, "the appalling fratricide of a nation gone mad." But since the focus is on the defenders, it is their courage, faith, and heroism that strikes the deepest chords. In one of the key scenes, the son of the rebel commander is captured by the "Reds." They deliver an ultimatum: Surrender or the son will be executed. The commandant refuses, in the name of saving Spain, and "the enemy took a diabolical pleasure in shooting the son within the hearing" of his father. In a note to producer Kenneth Macgowan, Levien wrote: "use loudspeakers for exchange between father & son...and then the Reds shooting the son near the loud speaker—the shot piercing every heart. I think that could be a deeply dramatic and moving scene." Franco arrives to save the last pocket of defenders from annihilation, and tells them, "You are the heroes and heroines of Spain....You typify the new Spain. Your heroism has attracted the attention and sympathy of the world, and your sufferings will not be in vain." In parentheses, Levien wrote "Fact."

A revised second treatment, co-written by Lamar Trotti, eliminated virtually all the scenes commenting on the civil war and opened with the commandant of the Alcazar making a dramatic speech of resistance and rebellion to his forces. It also eliminated Franco's speech. He is simply shown pinning a medal on the commandant. In fact, the second version, like all material facing the censorship office, was denuded of all the harsh facts of the war and virtually every political label, be it fascist, communist, red, etc. Even sanitized, the topic appeared too prone to controversy, and Zanuck scrubbed it.[47]

Levien was reassigned to help with a story about the great Chicago fire. Richard Collins and Niven Busch, working independently, had already written original stories. Busch was then given the green light to write a treatment, which Zanuck criticized for muddled characters and plots. Levien was told to work with Busch to simplify the storyline. The collaboration did not work. Macgowan wrote Zanuck:

> Miss Levien and Mr. Busch seem unable to agree on the detail of their work. I think you know that Busch has rather a lone-wolf, touchy temperament. Sonya says they have no personal friction. She leans towards characterization and he towards effective dramatic gags—which ought to make a good combination—but they can't get together on the detail of a story line. They have wasted so much time arguing that yesterday each started writing separately. Do you want them to continue or to do you want one or the other to drop out?

Zanuck ordered them to continue writing separately and he would determine the best treatment.

At a script conference on December 24, 1936, Zanuck announced that Levien's version suffered from too much atmosphere, Busch's from too little. He preferred Levien's prologue and Busch's establishment of the characters. But both had too many concurrent plots, did not focus enough on the central love story, and had weak conclusions. He ordered a single treatment combining the best of both versions and his comments. Both writers then produced lineups (scene summaries), and Levien's, with Busch's suggestions and amplifications, became the basis for a revised treatment that Zanuck liked very much. He assigned Lamar Trotti to work with Levien on the screenplay.

They worked well together, completing their first draft continuity in early March 1937, which tremendously pleased Zanuck with its flow and power. Costing $1.5 million to make, *In Old Chicago* earned $2.5 in domestic rentals alone, by far the studio's biggest grosser that year.[48]

Levien was then shifted to a costume drama having severe script difficulties, the adaptation of Robert Louis Stevenson's *Kidnapped*. Assigned to Macgowan at the end of 1936, he put Eleanor Harris and Curtis Kenyon to work on a synopsis and treatment. As per instructions, they introduced a love story. Zanuck did not like their work, because the screen story adhered too closely to the novel and seemed too contrived. He told the writers to use only the most exciting elements from the book and then invent freely.

He assigned Levien to collaborate with Harris on the rewrite. They restructured the novel, eliminating much of the odyssey through Scotland, concentrating the dramatic episodes, and strengthening the love story. Zanuck thought their treatment greatly surpassed the previous one but wanted more romance, a less contrived plot, and more modulated characters. When the first draft continuity did not satisfy his desire for more human characters, he assigned Ernest Pascal and Edwin Blum to rewrite it.

When the notice of tentative credits read "screenplay by Ernest Pascal and Edwin Harvey Blum, Sonya Levien and Eleanor Harris," Levien sharply challenged the studio. She wrote a single-spaced, five-page letter detailing her claim that she and Harris were responsible for "at least 75 percent of the work of preparing *Kidnapped* for the screen." She concluded that the claim of Pascal and Blum is "absolutely at variance with the facts." Finding this whole procedure "distasteful," she suggested a reversal of the teams. "I couldn't possibly accept second credit, and if this matter is arbitrated, I am certain that my contention will be upheld." The studio agreed, altering the credit to read: "screenplay by Sonya Levien, Eleanor Harris, Erwin Pascal and Edward Blum, based on the novel by Robert Louis Stevenson."[49] When the movie was exhibited, however, virtually every critic commented on Stevenson's tiny contribution to the finished product.

Levien then wrote what was for her an unusual script—a Hollywood story with a social conscience. An arrogant star who is presumed dead in an automobile accident had actually been saved by a Mexican family. Chastened by this experience, the star returns to Hollywood, a decent man, and is hired as a double to finish the film he had been working on at the time of the accident. As a nonstar, he sees the other side of Hollywood—"the small wage-earners' Hollywood, where every penny counts and where 'Trocadero' and 'Clover Club' are as remote as they would be to the residents of Kansas."[50] It was not produced.

The Falling Star script marked a general feeling of restlessness in Levien, a yearning, perhaps, to widen the scope of her writing. Blanche Knopf sent Levien several letters encouraging her to write a book about her experiences, but from the tone of Knopf's letters, it appears that Levien hesitated, unsure if she could do it. They apparently agreed that it would be in novel form, and a May 1941 letter to Levien indicates that she had written the first part of a book entitled *Russian Dateline*. But she did not send it to Knopf, who expressed disappointment that Levien had done no work on it. Four years after that, in 1945, Knopf sent her a contract, saying "I hope that it will give you the courage to go ahead and get under way with the book."[51]

Levien was also discussing the art of fiction with Mabel Dodge Luhan, now living in Taos, New Mexico. Luhan had inquired about the prospect of selling ideas to the movie studios, and Levien had encouraged her to try fiction. But, Levien warned, in fiction the author has to create the emotions of the characters. "That's hard—means terrific concentration and absorption on the characters until they are you."[52] Although she never wrote one, Levien believed that the novel was probably the most satisfying medium for a writer, probably because it offered the most complete control over the product.

By the end of 1937, Levien's star seemed to be dimming at the studio. Though Zanuck had increased production, he was assigning her fewer scripts. She had been loaned to Selznick International from August to November of 1937 to write an unproduced screenplay (*Merry, Merry Maidens*). Her screenplay for *Four Men and a Prayer* had required extensive rewriting. And she failed to satisfy Zanuck's desire for an antiwar movie based on Oscar E. Millard's *Libre Belgique,* the story of a World War I Belgian family's effort to publish a resistance newspaper in the face of ruthless German efforts to find and suppress it.

Unlike the brothers Warner, who were producing war-preparedness movies, Zanuck wanted to use *Libre Belgique* as a vehicle for his belief that power-seeking leaders fomented wars and manipulated soldiers into fighting them. He wanted an indictment against war and war lords. He also wanted it to be entertaining and instructed Levien to build up the family and love stories.

Levien faced two difficulties: weaving a coherent story from a source overcrowded with disconnected incidents and avoiding a characterization of Germans-as-occupiers that might anger the German government and lead it to close its markets to the studio's other movies. The legal department had advised her "to disguise all characters in her story" and "to depict all incidents in such a way that no reflections can be cast upon any of the [actual] characters involved."[53]

Sonya completed a treatment of *Uncensored* on March 17.

A few days later, Louella O. Parsons reported that studio executives were undecided about the project.

> The problem involved is the fact that it parallels in many ways the present situation in Austria, particularly the strict censorship of the press....The story in its present form is, of course, definitely anti-German and Twentieth Century-Fox will not produce it without careful thought.[54]

In her rewrite, Levien made two significant alterations. First, she rewrote the daughter's part "to suggest an exciting and dramatic role" for ice-skating star Sonja Henie. Second, she dropped the material depicting the German outrages.

> I have entirely omitted the German "heavy" angle by putting the burden of suppressing the uncensored paper upon a *Civilian*, a pompous, rather comic and unpopular gentleman whom the Kaiser appointed Chief Censor—and whom the German officers themselves look upon with contempt.[55]

But by the time she had completed the second treatment in December, Germany had taken control of the Sudetenland portion of Czechoslovakia, and studios began to scrub movies that appeared critical of Germany.

In between her two treatments of *Uncensored,* Twentieth had loaned Sonya to Samuel Goldwyn to assist in the rescue of a legendary script—*The Cowboy and the Lady.* Director Leo McCarey had related the germ of the idea to Goldwyn orally and then, in exchange for $50,000, provided a 25-page outline. McCarey then refused Goldwyn's offer to direct that "worthless piece of nothing." The script had almost as many titles as it had writers: *Spring Is in My Heart, A Kiss in the Sun, Howdy Stranger,* and *The Cowboy and the Heiress.* Since Paramount owned the copyright to the preferred title, *The Cowboy and the Lady,* and Goldwyn would not countenance *The Lady and the Cowboy*—giving Gary Cooper's role second billing—Goldwyn had to purchase the title rights from Paramount.

According to Garson Kanin, McCarey's outline was worthless—a treatment in need of a treatment. Fifteen writers undertook the sisyphean labor, among them Anita Loos and John Emerson, Lillian Hellman, Dorothy Parker and Alan Campbell. Robert Ardrey was then brought in from New York, with a $1,000 a week contract. He produced a rough draft and was then paired with S. N. Behrman, who had never worked on a Western before. "You write the cowboy, and I'll write the lady," he told Ardrey. Dissatisfied with the results, and perhaps at Behrman's suggestion, Goldwyn borrowed Levien from Twentieth. Robert Riskin then rewrote them, and Frank Ryan was assigned to the set to make last-minute revisions.

Goldwyn fired director William Wyler after two days, replacing him with H. C. Potter. Finally, with Behrman and Levien receiving screen credit, the ill-fated movie—costing nearly $2 million and starring Gary Cooper and Merle Oberon—opened. The *New York Times* reviewer noted that Goldwyn was "up to his knees in authors and abandoned scripts," but "the picture still seems to be in need of a final revision to bring it either more nearly into conformity or more ludicrously into non-conformity, with life as it is lived outside of movie studios."[56]

The script is notable for its commentary on American politics and its writers' queer view of it. The wealthy father of the heroine (Merle Oberon) is involved in a conspiracy of wealthy men to elect him president. She, dissatisfied with her father's world, retreats to Palm Beach to find the simpler life, goes out with two servant women, meets Stretch (Gary Cooper), and they marry. While he travels to his ranch to prepare it for her, she goes home to tell her father, who is in the midst of organizing his campaign for the presidency, and she delays telling him. During a banquet of the conspirators, Stretch arrives, but she does not acknowledge the marriage and allows the men to patronize him. Stretch then delivers a variant of Cooper's Robert Riskin/Frank Capra populist speeches:

> I'd advise you to get off your high-horse—and stop talking down to people. And the same goes for your smart-aleck friends here....I don't see where you get off to be pickin' anybody for President—when you haven't the decency to treat a person like a human being. Instead of inviting people to sit down at your table so you can laugh at them—maybe you better go and find out what they think and feel—and what their needs are—and how you can help them. In the long run that's all that's gonna count....I'd like to invite you all down to the ranch. Maybe we might be able to pound some decent manners into you.[57]

Stretch then stalks out. Fade in to the ranch, where daughter, then father, have journeyed, their lessons about love and ambition learned. Commenting on events throughout, with a Will-Rogers-like wryness, is the heroine's Uncle Hannibal.

Back at Twentieth, Levien was put to work on the adaptation of Walter D. Edmonds' lengthy, episodic novel, *Drums Along the Mohawk*. He later offered his "whole-hearted admiration" for her script. "I never could see a moving picture in the book, which has neither hero nor heroine in a dramatic sense, nor even a first rate part as I wrote it."[58] Bess Meredyth had made the first stab, producing a treatment in January 1937; William Faulkner had followed with a new treatment that July; and Levien finished her treatment in September 1938 and a first draft continuity in December.

Zanuck found her work too epical and flag-waving. She had included too many war and revolution scenes, thereby overshadowing the story he wanted told—about a pioneer boy and a city girl facing the problems of frontier life. In Short, he wanted a United States version of Pearl Buck's *The Good Earth*.

Lamar Trotti was given the rewrite assignment, but Zanuck found his effort confusing, bewildering, and lacking entertainment value. Levien's story line was more dramatic and conflict-laden, Zanuck decided, but he warned Trotti to omit all flag-waving episodes and any scenes portraying the British behaving brutally.

Trotti and Levien shared the credit. Zanuck praised her work—"sensational job. Brilliantly written"—and the movie brought in $2.2 million in domestic rentals (second on the studio's list that year).[59]

Levien wrote two more treatments for Twentieth before her tenure with the studio ended. After completing *Belle Starr*, she wrote to Zanuck that although she was sure she could think up still further ways of improving it, her main interest was writing the script for the next Irving Berlin picture,

> which I understand will have a "Tin-Pan Alley" background....[T]his is a field with which I am familiar. I was living in New York during the years "Tin-Pan Alley" developed and was at its most colorful, and I am a contemporary of the crowd that made it. Most of them, particularly Irving Berlin, are close friends of mine. I know their lives, their material, and their music.

She did not get the musical assignment, and her *Belle Starr* treatment received mixed reviews from studio readers. Niven Busch was assigned to write a new treatment, and Trotti wrote the final screenplay.[60] The studio readers also did not wax enthusiastic over her treatment for *Maryland*, a racehorse story for Walter Brennan that was designed to capitalize on the success of *Kentucky*.

As soon as the executives decided Sonya would not be assigned to the *Maryland* screenplay, they decided not to pick up her option for three more years at $1,800 a week. The studio's net operating profits were plummeting from $7.3 million to $1.1 million, and economy measures were in force. The previous December, eighteen writers had been released when they refused contract renewals pegged at their current weekly salary.[61] It is probable that the studio did not offer

Sonya a choice. In any event, her accumulated leave allowed the studio to put her on permanent layoff on May 20.

Three weeks later, on RKO Radio Pictures stationery, she wrote George Wasson, head of Twentieth's legal department, thanking him for his message of regret, and telling him:

> As it happens, it has worked out better for me—and probably for the studio also. Twelve [*sic*] in one spot is too long. I am working here now, writing *The Hunchback of Notre Dame*....I have another one here and then I go for two at M.G.M.[62]

RKO was paying Sonya $2,000 a week to write a screenplay based on Victor Hugo's *Notre Dame de Paris*. Her script was a model of cinematic adaptation. Like all Hugo's novels, *Notre Dame* slops over the edges, offering the reader many delightful detours into the social history of France, including disquisitions on city design, printing, and romanesque and gothic architecture. The main character is the cathedral and its denizens, individuals corrupted in a variety of ways. There is no redemption for any of them, and the innocents die unmourned.

Levien put the focus on Quasimodo (the hunchback who lived in the cathedral) and allowed the heroine, Esmeralda, to live and marry the hero, who loved her most truly. But Levien's script included much of the brutality, coarseness, and ugliness described by Hugo. In fact, the *New York Times* reviewer was dismayed at the "almost unrelievedly brutal" aspect of it (January 1, 1940). *Variety*, however, called it "a super thriller-chiller" (January 20).

Sonya also wrote a treatment for *The Enchanted Cottage*, an incredibly sappy story about love and physical appearance that RKO did not produce until 1945. (Based on a play by Arthur Wing Pinero, it had been adapted as a silent movie in 1924.)

Increasingly, Levien became absorbed in the events unfolding in Europe. During a two-week layoff from Twentieth in January 1939, she wrote a short story situated in Nazi Germany. *The New Yorker* rejected it, saying the ending "seems so very pat, and hence too artificial." Levien agreed, rewrote the ending, and sent it to *The New Statesman and Nation*, which accepted it but did not print it. Based on a true story, it centers on a German husband and wife who see a group of storm troopers rounding up and beating Jewish families.

> Frau Walden suddenly felt sick. It wasn't entirely due to compassion, but because fear, like a disease, is catching. That these wretched, terrified, huddling people were Jews did not lessen her fright. What if in a few months from now it were to be the Catholics? Or citizens who had French blood in their veins? Or all Germans who possessed more than a thousand gulden? This terrible callousness of one set of human beings for another filled her with horror.

Frau Walden's horror magnifies when she sees her son, Rudolph, kicking a young couple. Trying to break through the crowd to stop him, she is mistaken for a sympathizer or a Jewess and is spat upon and kicked.

When they relate the story to Rudolph, he is shocked to learn that they had tried to interfere to protect Jews. Expecting this response, his mother tells him about an event that occurred before his birth. She had discovered that Herr Walden had been having an affair, and she fled to Munich, where she would have died but for the care of a Jewish doctor. They fell in love, and she became pregnant. Herr Walden arrived, begged her forgiveness, accepted her pregnancy, and she decided to return to him. A contrite Rudolph resigns from the storm troopers and enrolls in medical school. The parents, of course, had fabricated the story.[63]

In December 1939, three months after the German invasion of Poland, Sonya wrote her English friend, F. Tennyson Jesse:

> I do not feel as sanguine as many of my friends do about the

German people. Most of them are behind Hitler, and are not going to revolt unless they are defeated. And I honestly believe they are for this war. They have a Jehovah complex that makes them want to be rulers of the world.[64]

The Hoveys supported United States involvement in the war. Carl would spend most of the war years working for the Office of War Information, while Sonya would sign her most lucrative contract to write screenplays for M-G-M.

Chapter 6

At M-G-M

Suffering from migraine headaches, released from her lucrative contract with Twentieth, her daughter about to leave for college in the East, war brewing in Europe, Sonya Levien seemed, for the first time, indifferent to her studio writing career. Only a few letters remain to provide her perspective on events, but Tamara Gold, her daughter, wrote a novel situated in the spring of 1940 that provides a perspective of the Hovey household.[1]

Naomi and Baxter Mull are husband and wife. Baxter possessed a "bony angularity of feature" and "an air of ease to his erect posture which had taken generations of disciplined spines at Boston dining tables to produce." Once a radical bohemian with a beard, he had long since abandoned both. He now displayed "short-lived but demonic bursts of temper" that unnerved everyone in the house. He responded to other's emotional outbursts by acting "the more calmly New England."

Christine, the daughter, had a vague knowledge of how, in his first years in California, "her father had tried time and again to get writing jobs and had failed until finally he had give up altogether, confining himself to long and unrealistic projects in his own study at home." He attended to the household chores and played a lot of tennis, while his manuscripts remained unfinished. Naomi blithely assigned him tasks on her way to the studio and "wondered with anguish how she would ever manage to train her husband not to treat her bank account cavalierly, as if it were an inexhaustible well."

Naomi, according to her daughter, would appear suddenly in rooms,

> like a small dark bird alighting from nowhere. There were no commas to [her] actions, never a moment that one could call repose. She gave the impression that the whole world was late for an appointment, and when one was with her one felt one ought to be rushing somewhere, accomplishing something vital.

Naomi frantically juggled her domestic responsibilities, devoting her full attention only to those problems requiring immediate solution. This tension, Christine thought, stemmed from the demands of the studio, where her mother "lived her real life as Naomi Barsky," and from a materially impoverished childhood. Perhaps it was memories of the latter that explained Naomi's insistence that Christine should attend Vassar or Bryn Mawr, where "You'll be known instantly as someone of real breeding," rather than the "undistinguished, dilettantish" Bennington.

Perhaps, Christine mused, Naomi seemed so sure of what her children should do because she had sheltered them far more than most mothers, "even from their own part-Jewishness," behind the convenient shield of Baxter's "unimpeachable Protestant New England heritage." Perhaps Naomi had shielded them as instinctively as she shielded herself from the pulverizing forces of a mainly male industry, where "any weakness she revealed would have been held, she always felt, against her sex or her origins." Economic necessity had provided her with "the kind of callous exterior one needed to work in Hollywood." Though she covered this callousness with a generous, agreeable plumage, Naomi harbored underneath a deep feeling of financial insecurity, an anxiety that

At M-G-M

her perch on the top rungs of the scriptwriting ladder could be lost and her economic position eradicated. "How many hundreds of times had she seen others lose their foothold in the industry over the past twenty years!...One lived on the edge of a precipice, partaking of luxuries but surrounded by a gulf of fear which paralyzed enjoyment."

Of course, Naomi's/Sonya's worst fears were not realized. Within days of her release from Twentieth, Pandro Berman brought her to RKO to write *Hunchback*—his last RKO production—and then brought her with him to M-G-M in May 1940 to produce a filmable script for a typical M-G-M musical extravaganza, *Ziegfeld Girl*.[2] Three scripts had been written for it since 1938, and Sonya was working on a "temporary incomplete" script in May when, suddenly, she gave up screenwriting. Six months later, she explained why to Fryn Harwood:

> I couldn't go on with picture writing. I had been working on a particularly trivial one when the news of Dunkirk evacuation came pouring in, and the subsequent fall of France. Suddenly, after listening to my radio, I got my hat and bag and left my office and never came back to it. There was nothing the matter with me, but suddenly my work seemed foolish and I couldn't go on.[3]

Marguerite Roberts did the revisions and they shared the screen credit.

She and Carl became active in the war preparedness movement, joining a group that sent letters and telegrams to senators and representatives, in Washington, asking them

> to do *something*, for America's own sake; but honestly, our efforts seem utterly futile. Most of America feels the way I do, but our form of government seems hopelessly muddled. We get 18 destroyers all ready for shipment and somebody digs up an old law which says it is unconstitutional.
> I can't write about it. I can only anguish and hate and

childishly pray for a plague to wipe out the whole Teutonic race.

She also wished "it were possible to bring over the children of France and England to America till the war is over." She wanted to provide homes for at least five.[4]

Levien spent the summer and early autumn in New York, where she became

> awfully involved with my family, and like the matriarch I have always been, got busy straightening out the lives of four married brothers. All with the best intentions. When I got through they disliked me for the first time and thoroughly. So I came back to California and felt much revived.[5]

She did some rewriting on *Ziegfeld Girl* and then spent "three wonderful months" at their Malibu beach house, writing an original story for Universal that was filmed as *The Amazing Mrs. Holliday*. The story continued her theme of individuals rescuing war-threatened children. A young American schoolteacher in China smuggles nine assorted children aboard a ship bound for San Francisco. The plot revolves around her efforts to get them into the country and the complications of a love affair. The script became a vehicle for Deanna Durbin. Sonya wrote Harwood:

> I like that way of working so much more that I have decided to free-lance and fill in between jobs with original stories written for the screen. Not as lucrative but less pressure. That is what I am beginning to mind—the awful pressure I have to work under at a studio.[6]

With Serge and Tamara in college and Carl in Washington, working for the Office of War Information, Sonya closed up the beach house, rented out the Rexford house, and leased the former Tom Mix mansion on Sunset Drive. The house was, she wrote Harwood, "a typical cowboy's dream of a castle.... Tom Mix is dead, but at night we hear him riding his horse right through the high-ceilinged drawing rooms and down the marble corridor. We have thought of turning the marble corridor into a skating rink and earning enough to keep the swimming pool going." When he was transferred to the OWI's Office of the Coordinator of Information in San Francisco and first saw the house, Carl wrote to Frances Perkins, "I don't know what we are doing in such a place—but that's Sonya."[7]

The Japanese attack on Pearl Harbor in December 1941 brought the United States into the war and Sonya called it "the greatest thing that could have happened to this nation.... It has solidified this country as nothing else on earth could have done." She felt some sympathy for the "loyal Japanese" in California who were about to be removed from their homes and placed in "relocation camps" but, like most Californians, she could not "help regarding them with suspicion."[8]

At some point in 1942, she decided to go back to studio work, signing a contract with Columbia Pictures. Nothing she wrote reached the screen, but at the end of the year, Columbia loaned her to Warner Bros. to work on a problem script there—a biography of George Gershwin. The scripting had begun in 1941, when Ira Gershwin agreed to spend eight weeks (at $1,875 each) talking to a screenwriter about his brother. Hal Wallis warned the head of the legal department to draw the contracts carefully, so that

> we have complete flexibility and the right to do any type of story we see fit. In other words, if we want to do the story of a composer, we do not want to be bound to follow the actual life of George Gershwin. We want full permission to fictionalize freely.[9]

Robert Rossen spent about two months on the project, Kathryn Scala another two, and then Clifford Odets devoted almost eight months to the script, completing it in October 1942. (His first version ran 800 pages, his revision 500.) According to Oscar Levant, the biggest script difficulty was in creating conflict—"there was almost none in George's life." Odets had him constantly torn between popular music and serious composing or, in Levant's words, Odets has "written his own life—but with song hits."[10] Dissatisfied with the script, on November 2 the new producer, Jesse Lasky, arranged to borrow Sonya from Columbia, reimbursing that studio her $1,000 a week salary. She worked until January 30, producing a new treatment. Considering how well she knew the Gershwins and their friends, Levien produced a remarkably flat account of George's life, lacking in psychological depth and character analysis. Three other writers worked on the script after she returned to Columbia: Harry Chandlee, Howard Koch, and Elliot Paul. She received an original story credit; Koch and Paul received screenplay credit.

The *Rhapsody* scriptwriting process revealed a characteristic problem in the business: apportioning money and credit for sources. Two writers of previous material on Gershwin claimed that their work had to have been used. The screenwriters, including Levien, swore they had not used these sources, but independent studio analyses indicated that material from both sources had been used, and both claimants received payment from Warner Bros.[11]

In 1943, Sonya signed a contract to write for M-G-M for $3,500 a week. According to Budd Schulberg, she was highly respected by the other writers, regarded "as a cut above the ordinary writer; one had a solid feeling about her, her presence, her mind at work." William Fadiman, who was then West Coast story editor for the studio, remembered her as a very hard- and fast-working writer.[12] Though M-G-M was a studio in decline, with its annual net profits and its percent share of industry profits nosediving, Carl described Sonya as "looking very young, as happy as can be.... This studio she likes best, because they have usually the best stories and stars."[13]

She was also, wrote Carl, "dotty" about her new grandson "and would sit and watch him for hours if her professional life did not happily intervene."[14] But a black cloud hovered in the form of a malignancy in Carl's throat. Sonya took him to the Mayo clinic, where his larynx was removed. For one year, he could not utter a sound, and for the rest of his life could only speak in a sort of croak. Forced to resign from the OWI, Carl began writing a biography of John Reed.

Back at M-G-M, Levien worked principally on adaptations of dramatic novels and musicals. The former did very well at the box office. *The Green Years* ranked sixth in 1946; *Cass Timberlane* sixth in 1948; *Quo Vadis* second in 1952. Her early musicals did less well. *Three Daring Daughters* ranked twenty-sixth in 1948 and *The Merry Widow* thirty-seventh in 1952, but she improved with *The Great Caruso* (fourth in 1952).

Sonya's first assignment at M-G-M was to adapt a novel about labor and management, Marcia Davenport's *The Valley of Decision*. The first writer, Anita Loos, had seen it as a parable about *noblesse oblige*, demonstrating that the privileges of being an American must be coupled with the duties of being an American. The Scott family, owners of a steel mill in Pittsburgh, do not "appreciate their situation or measure up to their birthright." The family servant, Mary, through her "high ideals and self-sacrifice," makes the family members worthy of their heritage. Dissatisfied with Loos's script, the studio assigned John Meehan and Sonya to write separate scripts that were then combined. Each continued to rewrite separately. The final screen story situates heroes and villains on both sides of a strike, but the clear weight of appreciation is for the benevolent, paternalistic owner and his one caring son. The moral of the story is that those owners who care deeply about their enterprises will do more for workers than anyone else.

The studio packaged the film brilliantly, making it a showcase for Greer Garson, their leading female star. The critics were less than enthusiastic. *The New Yorker* termed it "one of those big, glum pictures that always seem just about to say something but never quite get around to it" (May 17, 1945). The New York *Herald Tribune's* critic found it difficult to define the movie's social significance, noting "it does no violence to any cause any one might espouse" (May 4). The *New York Times* thought it had many elements of dramatic appeal but that Marcia Davenport's "fine American saga" had disappeared (May 4). Davenport, who had rejected M-G-M's offer to adapt her own novel, complimented the finished product and refused to express any disagreement or reservations.[15]

Only the Hollywood studio system could produce such an anodyne movie about labor-management relations in the midst of one of the bitterest strikes of the postwar period—a violent eight-month battle between the studios and the Conference of Studio Unions (CSU). The CSU, in its effort to democratize the union movement in the industry, had aroused the enmity of the studio bosses and the leaders of the largest (and most corrupt) union of studio workers, the International Alliance of Theatrical Stage Employees (IATSE). Using sweetheart tactics, red-baiting, and thuggery, the studios and the IATSE leadership conspired to destroy the CSU. Carl wrote Frances Perkins, "We have our own ideas about the right and wrong of it and not much hope that the right will come through. (Right stands for Left in this case!)"[16]

Sonya's second M-G-M assignment also involved a story with strong contemporary connotations. The story was based on Leonhard Frank's novel about France in the aftermath of World War I, *Karl und Anna*. Casey Robinson had written a script entitled *Beloved Stranger* that was given to Lester Cole and Levien for comments. Cole, a Communist deeply concerned about realistic treatment of movie topics, criticized the script for portraying the village in too placid, normal terms.

In fact, wrote Cole, there are long ration lines of hungry people everywhere in France. "There are," he continued, "numerous other examples of what amounts to complete unawareness of the grim, undernourished, heart-rending situation." It would be, he concluded, an insult to France to portray this village as slumbering contentedly in the newly arrived peace.

Levien had a different take, noting that she would "create a general re-line-up of the Casey Robinson script, with a few new sequences and added emotional values, which, I believe will enrich the story we are telling." Paired with her old friend Zoë Akins, the two worked on the renamed project—*A Woman of My Own*—for six months. They did not include Cole's suggestions. Two other writers revised and wrote retakes, and the final screen credit read screenplay by Marguerite Roberts and Zoë Akins; adaptation by Casey Robinson.[17]

Levien had an interesting experience on her third M-G-M script, adapting a novel written by her former lover, Sinclair Lewis. *Cass Timberlane* (1945) uses the trials and tribulations of an older man marrying a younger woman to comment on the vulgarity of the upper class in a Minnesota town. One of the worst written and least interesting of Lewis's novels, it had earned him far more than any other. It took five writers two years to transform the novel into a final shooting script. They had to make Cass a stronger presence, equal to Jinny, and they had to add some conflict outside the marriage, choosing a corruption trial involving Cass's upper-class friends, over which Cass presides.

Levien wrote a treatment and the studio brought in John O'Hara, at $1,000 per week, to produce a script. O'Hara came to the project bearing a strong animus toward Lewis, who had harshly panned O'Hara's *Appointment in Samara*. Thinking it was "a very bad" novel, O'Hara began by writing what he called "character profiles" of the four main roles, teasing out the psychological themes he would pursue in the script.

"The reason that I did it," he wrote later, "was that...by the time I was called in old Room Temperature [producer Arthur] Hornblow [Jr.] was all confusion about the characters and was passing on his confusion to Sonya Levien and me, and somebody had to start somewhere."

After spending two months on these "profiles," O'Hara and Levien, working separately, began turning in various scenes, sections, and notes. Hornblow thought that O'Hara's dialogue was awful, his blocking ineffective, and that he was, in effect, trying to demonstrate to Lewis how the novel should have been written. In fact, in the profile of Jinny, O'Hara wrote, "I think Lewis had a point here that eluded him." In any event, both writers were removed from the project in early 1946. Sidney Kingsley and Donald Ogden Stewart followed. In December, Levien and John Meehan were assigned to rewrite Stewart. They seem to have disagreed, and Levien ended up doing the final rewrites and changes. When the studio awarded co-screenplay credit to Stewart and Levien, Stewart objected and took the matter to a Screen Writers Guild arbitration hearing. The arbitrators decided that the screen credit should read, screenplay by Donald Ogden Stewart, adaptation by Stewart and Sonya Levien.[18]

Virtually simultaneously, Levien and Meehan were trying to salvage a silly musical, *Three Daring Daughters*. Going from the ridiculous to the sublime, she was next assigned to one of the studio's most troubled projects, *Quo Vadis?*, Henryk Synkiewicz's long, verbose, frequently tedious novel about love and Christianity in the age of Nero. It had been filmed in 1913 and 1925, and Irving Thalberg had purchased the rights from Universal in 1936.

The problem from the outset was to find a balance between the novel's three elements: love, faith, and tyranny. The first treatment of November 1936 had minimized Nero and his courtiers and focused on "the love story as written by the author, laid against the background of Christian persecution at the hands of Nero." The project was shelved until 1942, when Walter Reisch and Cyril Hume undertook it, to be followed by S. N. Behrman. Behrman and Reisch worked on it for seven months until July 1943, when it was again scrubbed.

In April 1948, Levien was assigned to critique the Behrman script. She decided that the script had departed too much from the novel in its rendering of key scenes, lacked dramatic contrasts and dealt too coldly with the love between Marcus and Lygia. She then produced a cut-and-paste script, interspersing her rewrites with the old Behrman screenplay and focusing on Nero's effort to crush Christianity. "A great deal of zeal and devotion went into the writing because I felt the story had a contemporary significance and message. Nero, Hitler, Mussolini, Stalin — are men of a kind." That autumn, with the rewritten script nearing completion, the project was assigned to Hornblow. Hugh Gray, a classics scholar, was brought in to comment on the verisimilitude of the rendering.

When John Huston was assigned to direct, he relied heavily on Gray to emphasize Nero's madness and cruelty and reduce the Christian scenes. Levien worked with them on the rewriting. But studio head Louis B. Mayer did not approve. He wanted an uplifting religious epic, and the new head of production, Dore Schary, who had no affinity with epics of any kind, sided with Huston. Rewrites by Levien and Gray continued throughout the rest of the year, but when leading man Gregory Peck's eye infection postponed the start of production, Hornblow and Huston asked to be relieved of their assignments. Their replacements, Sam Zimbalist and Mervyn LeRoy, brought in John Lee Mahin for a rewrite emphasizing the spectacular aspects of the novel. Mahin, Behrman, and Levien shared the screen credit.[19]

Sonya went directly from *Quo Vadis* to a biography of Enrico Caruso, the legendary tenor. A few months into the outline, she walked into William Ludwig's[20] office and told him she was struggling to find a dramatic thread. "I can't get the rhythm," she confessed. He conceived the theme that tied the movie together—the tenor's voice as double-edged sword opening the path to fame and closing it to everything else he wanted. They worked on it together for eight months. Dore Schary, the new head of production, liked their work, its "wonderful richness and flavor." Sonya wrote to Schary, "I have seldom had such deep convictions about the quality and popularity of a story, as I do about this. It has both glamour and human appeal—to the accompaniment of the most beautiful and stirring music in the world."

Nevertheless, she and Ludwig did not know how audiences would respond. Speaking about the first preview, she told a Books and Authors luncheon, "Mr. Ludwig and I...were in a very humble frame of mind when we arrived at the first preview." When the audience cheered and sang forth their "bravos," the writers "stood around with dazed expressions. We were the most surprised of all." Of the 417 cards handed in, 213 called it "outstanding" and 113 "excellent."[21]

The reviews for *The Great Caruso,* however, were not complimentary about the screenplay. Bosley Crowther wrote, "All the silliest, sappiest clichés of musical biography have been written by Sonya Levien and William Ludwig into the script" (*New York Times,* May 11, 1951). *Variety*'s reviewer found it "mawkish and trite" (April 18). The Screen Writers Guild nominated the script for its best written American musical award, and audiences liked the movie. During the first two weeks of its run, it outgrossed all M-G-M movies; its five week total was second only to *On the Town.*

Levien and Ludwig wrote four other musicals or musical biographies for M-G-M, *Oklahoma!* for an independent, and an unproduced musical for Columbia. Ludwig admired Sonya's intelligence and the way she used her demure looks to camouflage her determination to get what she wanted from the studio. "When I began to work with her," Ludwig told me, "most of the fire had gone out. Screenwriting was no longer that important a part of her life. It was just something that kept her busy. She wasn't very ambitious about it." She left early every day and avoided all story conferences. They would write separately, splitting the scenes, with him doing the comedy parts and any villains. Once a first draft was completed, he did all the revisions. When problems arose with directors or stars, he handled it. If they needed deeply personal information, such as for *Interrupted Melody*, he delved for it. But when it became necessary to convince the studio censor not to delete important scenes on the basis that they were risqué, Sonya's air of "motherly innocence" worked wonders. For example, she convinced the censors that an assignation in *The Merry Widow* was only a simple intimate dance.

Levien, however, thought she was working very hard. In late 1950, she wrote Mabel Dodge Luhan that she was suffering from hypertension and an enlarged heart caused by "the way I live. Always in a hurry both at the studio and home." A young writer, Joan Scott, who had become friends with Tamara and visited her at the beach house and the Tom Mix house, remembered that even on weekends Sonya was usually always working on a script.[22]

By this time, Sonya and Carl had moved from the mansion to a much smaller home on South Linden Drive. Along with Carl's deteriorating health, Sonya had to cope with an increasingly emotionally withdrawn Serge and the blacklisting of her daughter and son-in-law. Tamara, herself a screenwriter, had married screenwriter Lee Gold. They each had two credits when, on March 25, 1953, writer Sylvia Richards told the House Committee on Un-American Activities that she had been a member of radio and screenwriter Communist party branches along with Tamara Hovey and Lee Gold. They were not subpoenaed, but they were blacklisted and joined the Paris exile community, where Gold wrote two scripts for blacklisted director John Berry. There is nothing in the Levien papers on this event, and I have found no evidence indicating Levien's attitude toward the blacklist.

Meanwhile, work sustained her. Her and Ludwig's next two efforts, *The Merry Widow* and *The Student Prince*, received good notices from the reviewers. They slipped from the heights with *Hit the Deck* and then, in 1955, hit it big with *Interrupted Melody* and *Oklahoma!* Their script for *Interrupted Melody*, a biography of Australian opera singer Marjorie Lawrence, who made a dramatic comeback after being stricken with polio, received excellent notices from the reviewers, and Levien and Ludwig won the Academy Award for best story and screenplay. *Oklahoma!* was a huge box office success and earned a Writers Guild of America West nomination for best written American musical. Levien and Ludwig were the sole screenwriters for all those movies.

Sonya Levien may have been the most universally well-liked writer in the industry, Ludwig recalled. "I never heard anyone say a bad thing about her." When it was announced that she was to receive SWG's Laurel Award for lifetime achievement (1952), the audience responded with a roar of approval. In congratulatory telegrams, Jennings Lang wrote, "When your list of credits were announced, I saw before me the whole cavalcade of motion picture business....What survival in a profession where so many fall by the wayside." Richard Breen noted that collectively her pictures had grossed over $135 million. She herself, she wrote Quigley Productions in 1956, had "never been able to recollect all the pictures I have written in thirty-five years."[23]

Sonya's last script for M-G-M was *Bhowani Junction*, a strange topic for her. The novel by John Masters centered on love and cultural identity in a time of intense political turmoil. Masters commented that "I myself would not like to be faced with the task of putting [my novel] into the time and other limitations imposed on it by the movie medium," and the studio reader agreed. "This [book] is not tailor-made for films." Robert Ardrey spent six months writing a screenplay that did not satisfy the director, George Cukor. Levien wrote an outline for him in November 1954 and then began working with Ivan Moffat on the screenplay. Moffat, who had been recommended by George Stevens to add "an English idiom" to the script, found the story difficult to interpret and thought Levien lacked a feel for the subject matter and dialogue. While they were wrestling with it, Cukor went to Pakistan to begin filming, and the writers frequently had to write out of continuity to keep the director supplied with material. Cukor's letters about their work were consistently complimentary, and the writers joined him in England in March 1955, to continue writing and rewriting.[24]

Moffat described Levien as a "toiler, a workhorse," with strong shoulders, big forearms and wrists—"a peasant at the typewriter." She always seemed to be carrying a notebook and a fistful of sharpened pencils. She was, he continued, a timid-seeming woman, extraordinarily courteous. She never raised her voice or argued, acted in a near-servile fashion with supervisors, and treated courteously those who worked under her.

Moffat was very fond of Sonya but thought she lacked a sense of humor and a strong point of view. Her only desire was to make the script acceptable to the producer and director, to give them what they wanted exactly when they wanted it. She was, he concluded, "a perfect script butler." Though she knew the M-G-M hierarchy well and loved working at the studio, Sonya seemed to Moffat to harbor a great deal of professional anxiety. In London for the rewrites, she seemed to him obsessed with getting the script "right" and spent nights and weekends attempting to "battle through" the immense script problems.

Drastically recut by the studio so the love story swamped the politics, *Bhowani Junction* struck the reviewers as an uneven movie, though Bosley Crowther complimented the middle portion, which contained "a rapid, sure-fire rhythm of individual relationships which Sonya Levien and Ivan Moffat have clarified sharply out of [the novel]" (*New York Times*, May 25, 1956).

Sonya wrote one other script for M-G-M that might have made a fine extravaganza. It is one of her few scripts that is actually interesting to read. Adapted from Lion Feuchtwanger's historical novel *Raquel: The Jewess of Toledo*, the script depicts Sephardic culture in twelfth-century Spain, artfully interwoven with a love story and adventure scenes. Reading Feuchtwanger was no labor of love for Sonya. She wrote Fryn Harwood, "I thought I'd be inspired if I read his better novels. I find I sleep on them beautifully."[25]

In 1956, Sonya left M-G-M. Harry Cohn had hired director George Sidney from M-G-M to establish an independent production unit at Columbia Pictures and to serve as unofficial assistant head of production and heir apparent. Sidney brought Levien with him, giving her producer status. *The Hollywood Reporter* waxed eloquent over this move.

> They reached out and grabbed what they believe, and many others agree, is one of the most important writers in the business...who is not only a great writer but a great creator of stories and story ideas and has an executive ability that can and will develop some younger writers.[26]

Sidney produced *Pal Joey* and *The Eddie Duchin Story*, and Levien secured her last two writing credits for him: co-writer of the truly awful *Jeanne Eagels* and original story for *Pepe*. She wrote Harwood: "My hours are unbelievably long and I don't have much time for anything else...but I don't quarrel with this too much. I am still so bereft at the loss of Carl [June 25, 1956] that work is a godsend."[27] She had told an audience, either that year or the year before:

> A few days ago Harry Cohn asked me why I did not retire. I told him I could not think of anything I could do that would give me as much fun, excitement and surprises as writing for pictures. I should have added, with a bow to Samuel Hoffenstein, "and get a lousy fortune beside."[28]

Sonya continued, into her seventies, to produce scripts at an astonishing rate. She rewrote Clifford Odets' script, *Joseph and His Brethren*, for Louis B. Mayer (an independent producer after being fired by M-G-M); co-wrote an unproduced seaside love triangle; and co-wrote, for Samuel Bronston, a life of Jesus.[29]

Sonya Levien died March 19, 1960, leaving behind a record of credits and awards that likely will never be equalled. Not a great writer by any standards, she was a hugely successful writer by every standard, soaring ever upward from immigrant factory girl on New York's Lower East Side to one of Hollywood's highest-paid, most-rewarded writers. Along the way, she jettisoned her political attitudes and desire for a large nuclear family but compensated by nurturing a huge extended kinship group deeply loyal to her. She was indeed a, perhaps *the*, great lady of Hollywood.

Endnotes

Preface

1. For a discussion of books on screenwriters, see my review in *Cineaste* 18, no. 4 (nd), 53-55.

2. The first two substantial overviews appeared last year: Lizzie Francke, *Script Girls: Women Screenwriters in Hollywood* (London: British Film Institute, 1994) and Marsha McCreadie, *The Women Who Write the Movies: From Frances Marion to Nora Ephron* (New York: Birch Lane, 1994).

3. The published biographical material on her is sparse. The main source is Edith Hurwitz, "Sonya Levien," *Dictionary of Literary Biography* 44, *American Screenwriters*, Second Series (Detroit: Gale Research Company, 1986), 171-78. It is mainly based on studio publicity releases and serves, in turn, as the main basis for Alley Acker, *Reel Women: Pioneers of the Cinema, 1896 to Present* (New York: Continuum, 1991), 189-92. A sparse clipping file is at the Margaret Herrick Library, Academy of Motion Picture Arts and Sciences, and a large archive of letters and scripts is held by the Huntington Library (San Marino, CA). (The Huntington recently recatalogued this collection, but the curators have not prepared a new index.) The Division of Rare Books and Special Collections, University of Wyoming Library, has eight scripts written between 1939 and 1956, but all of them are available at the Huntington or Herrick libraries.

Chapter 1

1. The most detailed historical sources of life in the Pale are in Yiddish, which I cannot read. I have derived this summary from the following English-language sources: Abraham Cahan, *The Education of Abraham Cahan*, Leon Stern, et al., trans. (Philadelphia: Jewish Publication Society of America, 1969); Israel Cohen, *Vilna* (Philadelphia: Jewish Publication Society of America, 1943); Simon M. Dubnow, *History of the Jews in Russia and Poland: From the Earliest Times until the Present Day*, I. Friedlaender, trans., vol. 2 (Philadelphia: Jewish Publication Society of America, 1918); Avraham Kariv, *Lithuania: Land of My Birth* (New York: Herzl Press, 1967); Nora

Levin, *While Messiah Tarried: Jewish Socialist Movements, 1871-1917* (New York: Schocken, 1977); Ezra Mendelsohn, *Class Struggle in the Pale: The Formative Years of the Jewish Workers' Movement in Tsarist Russia* (Cambridge: Cambridge University Press, 1970); Nancy Schoenburg and Stuart Schoenburg, *Lithuanian Jewish Communities* (New York: Garland, 1991).

2. Cahan, *The Education of Abraham Cahan*, 6-8.
3. Kariv, *Lithuania*, 10.
4. Levin, *While Messiah Tarried*, 29.
5. Mendelsohn, *Class Struggle in the Pale*, 38.
6. George Woodcock, *Anarchism: A History of Libertarian Ideals and Movements* (Cleveland: Meridian, 1962), 399-410. For biographies of Kropotkin, see George Woodcock and Ivan Avakumovic, *The Anarchist Prince: A Biographical Study of Peter Kropotkin* (Boston: Schocken, 1971) and Martin A. Miller, *Kropotkin* (Chicago: University of Chicago Press, 1976). Also see Peter Kropotkin, *Memoirs of a Revolutionist* (Boston: Houghton Mifflin, 1899).
7. Cahan, *The Education of Abraham Cahan*, 145, 149, and 158. See also A. L. Patkin, *The Origins of the Russian-Jewish Labour Movement* (Melbourne: F. W. Cheshire, 1947).
8. Alida S. Malkus, "She Came to America from Russia: The Story of Sonya Levien," *Success* (January 1925), 55-57 and 121.
9. Interview with Budd Schulberg. He thinks his mother acted as Levien's Hollywood agent for a few years.
10. Sonya Levien to Father James Keller, January 24, 1952, Sonya Levien papers, Huntington Library.
11. Kariv, *Lithuania*, 63.
12. Sonya Levien, "The Franks Case Makes Me Wonder," *Hearst's International Magazine* (December 1924), 18. *Talmud* is the written version of orally transmitted interpretations and applications of *Torah*. The *Shulhan Arukh* (Prepared Table), a digest of Jewish law composed by Joseph ben Ephraim Caro (1488-1575), eliminated all exhortation and theological interpretation. See Robert M. Seltzer, *Jewish People, Jewish Thought: The Jewish Experience in History* (New York: Macmillan, 1980), 460.
13. These and other statistics are to be found in the Appendix to Samuel Joseph, *Jewish Immigration to the United States, from 1881 to 1910* (New York: Columbia University Press, 1914). The Leviens were missed by the 1900 census, and the 1910 census is virtually impossible to use without an exact street address. So these dates stem from information in the 1920 census, when Julius, Fanny, Nathan, and Edward were living in the Bronx. By then, Julius was a jobber in cloaks. I was unable to locate their naturalization papers.
14. Robert E. Hewes, "Noted Writer in Hollywood," *Hollywood Daily Citizen* (December 27, 1921), 1 and 7.
15. Melech Epstein, *Jewish Labor in U.S.A.: An Industrial, Political and*

Cultural History of the Jewish Labor Movement, 1882-1914 (NP: KTAV, 1969), 1:215-17; Paul Avrich, *Anarchist Portraits* (Princeton, NJ: Princeton University Press, 1988), 192; Peter Kropotkin, "Anarchism: Its Philosophy and Ideal," in Roger N. Baldwin, ed., *Kropotkin's Revolutionary Pamphlets: A Collection of Writings by Peter Kropotkin* (New York: Blom, 1927), 137. In the Levien papers there is a collection of typed copies of some letters of anarchist speaker, writer, and activist Emma Goldman, given to Levien by John G. Moore at some point in the late 1920s. No explanation for this gift was provided. Also in the Levien papers are letters from Alexandra Kropotkin, daughter of the anarchist theorist. In the opening letter, April 4, 1931, Kropotkin indicates that she and Levien had met and become friendly and then had lost contact.

16. Levien to Henry Kitchell Webster, August 6, 1917, Levien papers; Hewes, "Noted Writer in Hollywood." According to Emanuel Hertz: "Time was when a great portion of Russian Jews could be found in the Socialist and Anarchist camps....But as time went on, as prosperity dawned on them, they gradually drifted" into mainstream political parties. Charles S. Bernheimer, ed., *The Russian Jew in the United States* (Philadelphia: Winston, 1905), 266-67.

17. Sonya Levien, "In the Golden Land," *The Metropolitan* (April 1918), 8.

18. Levien, "The Franks Case," 107.

19. Stephan F. Brumberg, *Going to America, Going to School: The Jewish Immigrant Public School Encounter in Turn-of-the-Century New York City* (New York: Praeger, 1986). See also Henrietta Szold, "The Education of the Jewish Girl," *The Maccabaean* 5 (July 1903), 10.

20. *Forward* (August 8, 1905), quoted in Irving Howe, *World of Our Fathers* (New York: Harcourt Brace Jovanovich, 1976), 266.

21. *Autobiography of Rose Pastor Stokes,* 1899-1915, incomplete second draft, 108-109, Rose Pastor Stokes papers, group 573, series II, box 6, folder 6c, Manuscripts and Archives, Yale University Library. See also Arthur Zipser and Pearl Zipser, *Fire and Grace: The Life of Rose Pastor Stokes* (Athens, GA: University of Georgia Press, 1989). The University Settlement, founded as the Neighborhood Guild (1886), was designed to narrow the gap between the professional and laboring classes. It functioned as an agency of assimilation and endeavored to resolve social class problems in a peaceful manner. See Harry P. Kraus, *The Settlement House Movement in New York City, 1886-1914* (New York: Arno, 1980), 63.

22. In 1917, Stokes wrote Levien, "you seem a *part* of my life.... You were bound up with so much of it." And Levien, in 1927, wrote a mutual friend, "I have always loved Rose and it hurts me to think that we have just lost track of each other." Eleven years later, Levien wrote, "the memory of Rose is still strong in my heart." Stokes to Levien, November 11, 1917, Levien papers; Levien to Philip Russ, [September or October 1927], Rose Pastor

Stokes papers, Tamiment Collection, Bobst Library, New York University; Levien to Lillian Pastor Fletcher, February 2, 1938, Levien papers.

23. Diane Heckert, "Prize-Winning Movie Scripter," *Dayton Daily News* (November 30, 1954), clipping in Levien papers. Since Levien had not been graduated from a four-year high school, she could not enroll as an L.L.B. candidate. She took the same courses, however. In her graduating class, she was the only women among twenty-eight. Eleven other women earned L.L.B. degrees from N.Y.U. that year.

24. Typed manuscript, no date, Levien papers.

25. Levien to Edgar L. Sisson, January 31, 1911, and unsent, handwritten draft, both in Levien papers. It is not clear why she chose *Collier's*, save that it represented a giant commercial step above *Success* and contained a "Woman To-Day" page.

26. Flora Merrill, "Sonya Levien Made Sacrifices to Have a Career," *New York World* (June 28, 1925), 6M, and *Boston Sunday Post* (July 5, 1925), B3.

27. Levien to Friedman, December 4, 1953, and December 10, 1957, Levien papers. Friedman helped edit *The Man from Main Street: Selected Essays and other Writings* (London: Heinemann, 1954). Mark Schorer, *Sinclair Lewis: An American Life* (New York: McGraw-Hill, 1961), 193. Thirty-five years later, Lewis criticized Levien's adaptation of his novel *Cass Timberlane* (M-G-M, 1947).

28. Malkus, "She Came to America"; Ludwig interview with author. In November 1911, she received an invitation to join The Women's Lawyers' Club, which published a journal and lobbied for legislation favorable to women and children. Levien papers.

29. *The Woman's Journal* (October 5, 1912, 316). The letters are in Levien papers. Very few Jewish women achieved important executive positions in the woman suffrage organizations, although Jewish people strongly supported the movement. See Elinor Lerner, "Jewish Involvement in the New York City Woman Suffrage Movement," *American Jewish History* 70 (June 1981), 442-61.

30. S. N. Behrman, *Tribulations and Laughter: The Memoirs of S. N. Behrman* (London: Hamish Hamilton, 1972), 180. During her short tenure at *The Woman's Journal*, it printed an article by Hovey suggesting that women could be a force for socializing the police department and humanizing policemen. Carl Hovey, "Women and the Police," *The Woman's Journal* (July 27, 1912), 240.

31. Justin Kaplan, *Lincoln Steffens: A Biography* (New York: Simon and Schuster, 1974), 82-88; Lincoln Steffens, *The Autobiography of Lincoln Steffens* (New York: Literary Guild, 1931), 311-16; Hutchins Hapgood, *A Victorian in the Modern World* (New York: Harcourt, Brace, 1939), 138-41.

32. Carl Hovey, *The Life Story of J. Pierpont Morgan: A Biography* (Toronto: Copp Clark, 1911).

Chapter 2

1. Mabel Dodge Luhan, *Movers and Shakers* (Albuquerque, NM: University of New Mexico, 1985), 85. Hovey attended some of her "evenings" and exchanged notes with her regularly on various literary topics. He and Sonya visited Luhan in Taos in 1937. See Lois Palken Rudnick, *Mabel Dodge Luhan: New Woman, New Worlds* (Albuquerque, NM: University of New Mexico Press, 1984).

2. *The Metropolitan* (March 1912), 4. Hovey was named managing editor in May 1913; Sonya became the fiction editor one month later. They looked for "the sincere story," one that contained "real observation." Carl Hovey, "Fiction from an Editorial View-point" (August 1914), 2.

3. Ibid. (June 1912), 6.

4. Ibid. (August 1912), 6.

5. Ibid. (September 1912), 6.

6. Ibid. (April 1913), 4.

7. Ibid. (March 1913), 45-46.

8. Charlotte Perkins Gilman, *The Living of Charlotte Perkins Gilman* (New York: Appleton-Century, 1935; New York: Arno, 1972), 313. See also Judith Schwarz, *Radical Feminists of Heterodoxy: Greenwich Village, 1912-1940* (Lebanon, NH: New Victoria, 1982). Three of Gilman's articles on feminism had appeared in *Success* during Levien's tenure.

9. Sonya Levien, "An Introduction to the Militant Camp," *The Metropolitan* (October 1913), 25-26.

10. See Frederic C. Howe, *The Confessions of a Reformer* (New York: Charles Scribner's Sons, 1925), 240.

11. Sonya Levien, "Sentimental New York," *The Survey* (January 4, 1913), 415-16.

12. Memo dated October 24, 1913, Levien papers.

13. Sonya Levien, "New York's Motion Picture Law," *The American City* 9 (October 1913), 319-21.

14. Sonya Levien, "Women in War (By a Spectator)," *The Little Review* (September 1914), 4-5.

15. Sonya Levien, "Would Women Do Away with War?" *The Metropolitan* (June 1915), 43.

16. Ibid. (July 1917), 6.

17. Tamara Hovey, *John Reed: Witness to Revolution* (New York: Crown, 1975), 153-54. See also Granville Hicks, *John Reed: The Making of a Revolutionary* (New York: Macmillan, 1937); Richard D. O'Connor and Dale L. Walker, *The Lost Revolutionary: A Biography of John Reed* (New York: Harcourt, Brace and World, 1967); and Robert A. Rosenstone, *Romantic Revolutionary: A Biography of John Reed* (New York: Knopf, 1975).

Actually, Hovey fired Reed three months before the president asked Congress for a declaration of war and six months before the administration began its crackdown on publications critical of the war effort.

18. Transcript of tape made for the Theodore Roosevelt Centennial, October 1957, Levien papers; Sonya Levien, "The Great Friend: A Personal Story of Theodore Roosevelt as he revealed himself to one of his associates in magazine work," *Woman's Home Companion* (October 1919), 7-8 and 104. See also Joseph L. Gardner, *Departing Glory: Theodore Roosevelt as ex-President* (New York: Charles Scribner's Sons, 1973).

19. Robert E. Hewes, "Noted Writer in Hollywood," *Hollywood Daily Citizen* (December 27, 1921), 1 and 7.

20. The letters, dated September 1 and September 7, 1917, and October 11, 1918, are in the Mary Austin papers, folders 1128, 1130, and 3471, Huntington Library. Their correspondence does not seem to have continued with any regularity. One year later, Levien sent all their correspondence on psychic matters to Mabel Dodge. Dodge and Austin had known each other since 1913, and Austin would settle in Santa Fe about the same time Dodge settled in Taos. Together they fought to preserve native art and culture from ruinous legislation. See Esther Lanigan Stineman, *Mary Austin: Song of a Maverick* (New Haven, CT: Yale University Press, 1989).

21. Interview with William Ludwig.

22. Interview with Robert Levien.

23. Sonya Levien, "The Franks Case Makes Me Wonder," *Hearst's International* (December 1924), 18.

24. Sonya Levien, "In the Golden Land," *The Metropolitan* (April 1918), 8.

25. Day's letters to Levien, virtually all undated, are in Levien papers. Day, Sr., was a stockbroker, and the younger Day purchased stocks for her and sent her investment advice.

26. Sonya Levien, "Why I Decline Stories," *The Writer's Monthly* (November 1921), 387-95.

27. Sonya Levien, "My Pilgrimage to Hollywood," *The Metropolitan* (September 1922), 36 and 114.

28. Several other contributors to *The Metropolitan* also sent their work and then themselves to Hollywood: Rupert Hughes, Mary Roberts Rinehart, Anzia Yezierska, Zoë Akins, F. Scott Fitzgerald, Louis Weitzenkorn, William S. McNutt, and Ben Hecht.

Chapter 3

1. Benjamin Hampton, *History of the American Film Industry: From Its Beginnings to 1931* (New York: Dover, 1970), 248 and 313. Originally published as *A History of the Movies* (New York: Covici, Friede, 1931).

Endnotes

2. Lewis Jacobs, *The Rise of the American Film* (New York: Harcourt, Brace, 1939), 265-66, 268, 271, and 277.

3. Hampton, *History of the American Film Industry*, 219-20 and 249.

4. Frances Marion, *Off With Their Heads! A Serio-Comic Tale of Hollywood* (New York: Macmillan, 1972), 64.

5. Kevin Brownlow, *Behind the Mask of Innocence* (New York: Knopf, 1990), xv-xix.

6. Richard Koszarski, *An Evening's Entertainment: The Age of the Silent Feature Picture, 1915-1928*, vol. 3 of *History of the American Cinema*, Charles Harpole, gen. ed. (New York: Scribner's 1990), 181 and 184.

7. Jesse L. Lasky, with Don Weldon, *I Blow My Own Horn* (Garden City, NY: Doubleday, 1957), 129.

8. Marion, *Off With Their Heads!*, 94.

9. Kristin Thompson, "The Formulation of the Classical Style, 1909-28," in David Boardwell et al., *The Classical Hollywood Cinema: Film Style & Mode of Production to 1960* (New York: Columbia University Press, 1985), 165.

10. Lasky, *I Blow My Own Horn*, 133.

11. Hampton, *History of the American Film Industry*, 209.

12. Ibid., 307.

13. Janet Staiger, "The Hollywood Mode of Production to 1930," in Boardwell, *The Classical Hollywood Cinema*, 138.

14. Kenneth Macgowan, "The March of the Photoplay," *Motion Picture Classic* (May 1919), 17 and 71.

15. Frederick James Smith, "The Low-Brow Playwright Speaks," *Motion Picture Classic* (August 1920), 26 and 80.

16. Hampton, *History of the American Film Industry*, 309-10.

17. Barbara Beach, "The Scenario's the Thing," *Motion Picture Classic* (September 1919), 20 and 78.

18. Frederick James Smith, "Truth on the Screen," *Motion Picture Classic* (April 1921), 36 and 75. See also Clara Beranger, "Good and Bad Authorship," ibid. (September 1923,) 78; and Avery Strakasch, "Elinor Glyn on the Technique of the Scenario," ibid. (October 1923), 34 and 78-79.

19. Carl Hovey, "The Moving Picture Moves," *The Bookman* 63 (May 1926), 281-84.

20. Kenneth Macgowan, *Behind the Screen* (New York: Delacorte, 1965), 383 and 380. *Variety* (November 4, 1935) reported that in the production year ending October 1, 1935, the major studios produced 301 feature-length movies, with 509 writers receiving some form of screen credit.

21. F. Scott Fitzgerald, *The Last Tycoon* (New York: Charles Scribner's Sons, 1941), 58.

22. Donald Ogden Stewart, "Writing for the Movies," *Focus on Film* 5 (Winter 1970), 52.

23. Leo Rosten, *Hollywood: The Movie Colony, the Movie Makers* (New York; Harcourt, Brace, 1941), 306 and 310.

24. Deposition of Lester Cole, *Cole v. Loew's, Inc.*, United States District Court, Southern District of California, No. 8005-Y, September 10 and 11, 1948, 54-5.

25. United States, National Recovery Administration, *Report Regarding Investigation Directed to Be Made by the President in His Executive Order of Fair Competition for the Motion Picture Industry*, prepared by Sol A. Rosenblatt, July 7, 1934 (Washington, D.C.: USGPO, 1934), 24; *Variety* (November 4, 1935), 11; (February 29, 1940), 1 and 5; (October 14, 1943), 1 and 6.

26. Gerald Mast, *A Short History of the Movies*, 5th ed., revised by Bruce F. Kawin (New York: Macmillan, 1992), 132.

27. John Emerson and Anita Loos, *How to Write Photoplays* (New York: McCann, 1920), 2-3, and *Breaking Into the Movies* (New York: McCann, 1921).

28. Anthony Slide, *Early Women Directors* (New York: Da Capo, 1984), 9-13.

29. Carolyn Lowrey, *The First One Hundred Noted Men and Women of the Screen* (New York: Moffat, Yard, 1920), 118.

30. See Nell Shipman, *The Silent Screen and My Talking Heart: An Autobiography* (Boise, ID: Boise State University, 1987).

31. Ally Acker, *Reel Women: Pioneers of the Cinema, 1896 to Present* (New York: Continuum, 1991), xxv. Dorothy Calhoun identified another species of predominant female—movie mothers. "The strain of keeping up with their famous offspring seems to have been too much for male parents. And so the producers, instead of dealing with their own sex when it comes to talking contracts, find themselves confronted with middle-aged ladies whose natural maternal pride has been magnified into the conviction that they have the most talented and beautiful children in the world. Chivalry forbidding the shaking of fists and waving of hands, the producers are rendered speechless, while the ladies have the final unanswerable argument of tears." Dorothy Calhoun, "Do Women Rule the Movies?" *Motion Picture Classic* (August 1928), 30.

32. Pat McGilligan, ed., *Backstory: Interviews with Screenwriters of Hollywood's Golden Age* (Berkeley, CA: University of California Press, 1986), 143.

33. Marion, *Off With Their Heads!*, 185.

34. *Who Wrote the Movie and What Else Did He Write?* (Los Angeles: Academy of Motion Picture Arts and Sciences and Writers Guild of America West, 1970). Between 1936-60, women constituted 12 percent of Screen Writer Guild (Writers Guild of America) membership. When it came time to elect officers, women did not receive strong consideration. Six served as vice-president, one as secretary, and one as president (three terms). The latter, Mary McCall, Jr., was the only woman officer between 1938-60. In some years, a woman was not represented on the board, and overall they held less than 10 percent of board positions.

35. Nell Shipman, "Me," *Photoplay* (February 1919), 47-48.

36. Anita Loos, *Cast of Thousands* (New York: Grosset & Dunlap, 1977), 19-25.
37. Marion, *Off With Their Heads!*, 13-33.
38. Lenore Coffee, *Storyline: Recollections of a Hollywood Screenwriter* (London: Cassell, 1973), 12-71.
39. Lowrey, *The First One Hundred*, 52.
40. Marion, *Off with Their Heads!*, 83.
41. Malcolm Cowley, ed., *Writers at Work: The Paris Review Interviews* (New York: Viking, 1958), 81.
42. Interview with William Ludwig; Mary Ellin Barrett, *Irving Berlin: A Daughter's Memoir* (New York: Simon and Schuster, 1994), 80.
43. Interview with Bess Taffel.
44. Patrick McGilligan, *George Cukor: A Double Life* (New York: St. Martin's, 1991), 89.
45. Sonya Levien, "My Pilgrimage to Hollywood," *The Metropolitan* (September 1922), 36 and 114.
46. Sonya Levien, "The Screen Writer," in Catherine Filene, ed., *Careers for Women: New Ideas, New Methods, New Opportunities — to Fit a New World*, rev. ed. (Boston: Houghton Mifflin, 1934), 433-37.
47. Levien to Mabel Dodge Luhan, September 12, 1937, Levien papers.

Chapter 4

1. Sonya Levien, "My Pilgrimage to Hollywood," *The Metropolitan* (September 1922), 36 and 114.
2. Paramount Collection, Margaret Herrick Library.
3. Ibid.
4. Levien, "My Pilgrimage."
5. Robert E. Hewes, "Noted Writer in Hollywood," *Hollywood Daily Citizen* (December 27, 1921), 1 and 7.
6. Salary and cost figures are in the legal files of the Paramount Collection.
7. Alida Malkus, "She Came to America from Russia: The Story of Sonya Levien," *Success* (January 1925), 55-57, 121.
8. Ibid.
9. For biographical details, see Anzia Yezierska, *Red Ribbon on a White Horse* (New York: Charles Scribner's Sons, 1950); Carol B. Schoen, *Anzia Yezierska* (Boston: Twayne, 1982); and Louise Levitas Henriksen, *Anzia Yezierska: A Writer's Life* (New Brunswick, NJ: Rutgers University Press, 1988). For her stories, see *Hungry Hearts and Other Stories*, Louise Levitas Henriksen, ed. (New York: Persea, 1985) and *How I Found America: Collected Stories of Anzia Yezierska*, Vivian Gornick, ed. (New York: Persea, 1991).
10. Anzia Yezierska, "This Is What $10,000 Did to Me," *Cosmopolitan*

(October 1925), reprinted in *Hungry Hearts and Other Stories*, 299-315. She tells the same story, in greater detail, in *Red Ribbon*.

11. The story of Yezierska's experience with *Hungry Hearts* is in Kevin Brownlow, *Behind the Mask of Innocence* (New York: Knopf, 1990), 396-403, and Henriksen, *Anzia Yezierska*, 164-67.

12. Paramount Collection.

13. Neither in the Levien papers nor the Anzia Yezierska Collection (Special Collections, Mugar Memorial Library, Boston University) are there letters from one to the other.

14. Undated New York *Journal* review is in the clipping file, Herrick Library.

15. Sonya Levien, "The Franks Case Makes Me Wonder," *Hearst's International* (December 1924), 18-19 and 107-108.

16. F. Tennyson Jesse and H. M. Harwood, *London Front: Letters Written to America, 1939-1940* (New York: Doubleday, Doran, 1941), 83.

17. Lehr to Levien, June 11, 1925, Levien papers

18. Day to Levien, August 27, [1925?], ibid.

19. S. N. Behrman, *Tribulations and Laughter: A Memoir* (London: Hamish Hamilton, 1972), 140, 142, and 179. De Mille had offered Hovey an eight-week contract at $150 per week and three yearly options. The offer included transportation to Los Angeles and back to New York if the first option was not exercised. In 1926, in response to a *New Yorker* form letter asking for "Profiles," he proposed five subjects and received approval to do three (D. W. Griffith, Jesse Lasky, and Mary Roberts Rinehart). None appeared. She proposed William Fox and Joseph Schenck, but then decided not to do them. Levien papers.

20. Libbian Benedict, "The Story of Sonya Levien," *The American Hebrew*, (June 19, 1925), 207.

21. Flora Merrill, "Sonya Levien Made Sacrifices to Have a Career," New York World (June 28, 1925) 6M, and *Boston Sunday Post* (July 5, 1925), B3.

22. Sonya Levien, "Doubling in Love," Los Angeles *Times Sunday Magazine* (December 25, 1927), 4-5 and 25. The program and review of *By the Sword* is in Levien papers. I have not found a synopsis of her other play, *The Jewish Millionaire*.

23. Day to Levien, November 20, 1927, ibid.

24. Levien worked with sociologist John Collier at the People's Institute (he had created and directed its National Board of Censorship) and socialized with him at Mabel Dodge's salon. Although he was deeply impressed by Kropotkin's *Mutual Aid*, I have found no indication that he painted or drew. Collier by that time had moved west and become the leading campaigner for Indian reform legislation. See his *From Every Zenith: A Memoir and Some Essays on Life and Thought* (Denver, CO: Sage, 1963).

25. Written as "His Country, " it is in Levien papers.

26. Levien to Chandler Sprague, March 20, 1928, ibid.

27. Levien to Selznick, March 28, 1928, ibid.
28. Written as "Goldfish," ibid.
29. Frank Capra, *The Name Above the Title: An Autobiography* (New York: Macmillan, 1971), 450.
30. Lenore Coffee, *Storyline: Recollections of a Hollywood Screenwriter* (London: Cassell, 1973), 190-94.

Chapter 5

1. Kevin Brownlow, *Behind the Mask of Innocence* (New York: Knopf, 1990), 255.
2. Gordon Allvine, *The Greatest Fox of Them All* (New York: Stuart, 1969), 81-82; James R. Quirk, "How to Become a Great Producer," *Photoplay* (July 1928), 45, 119-120; Aubrey Solomon, *Twentieth Century-Fox: A Corporate and Financial History* (Metuchen, NJ: Scarecrow, 1988).
3. Benjamin B. Hampton, *History of the American Film Industry: From its Beginnings to 1931* (New York: Dover, 1970), 336-38.
4. Sonya Levien file, Twentieth Century-Fox Film Corp. legal records, UCLA Arts Library-Special Collections.
5. S. N. Behrman, *Tribulations and Laughter: A Memoir of S. N. Behrman* (London: Hamish Hamilton, 1972), 138-43.
6. In the Sonya Levien biography file, Margaret Herrick Library.
7. Sonya Levien to William Crawford, June 19, 1930, Twentieth legal records. The legal department claimed it had not received her assignments—forms signed by a writer after completing work on a script—for these movies.
8. Catherine Filene, ed., *Careers for Women: New Ideas, New Methods, New Opportunities to Fit a New World*, rev. ed. (Boston: Houghton Mifflin, 1934), 435-36; see also Levien to Catherine Filene Shouse, April 7, 1933, Levien papers.
9. Flora Merrill, "Sonya Levien Made Sacrifices to Have a Career," *New York World* (June 28, 1925), 6M.
10. Bolton quoted in "Bio" ; Levien to Joseph Verner Reed, April 5, 1935, both in Levien papers.
11. Telegram dated June 13, 1928, *Behind that Curtain* file, Twentieth Century-Fox legal records. One of Der Biggers' stories had appeared in *The Metropolitan* during Levien's tenure as fiction editor.
12. See John Relton, *The Hollywood Professionals: Howard Hawks, Frank Borzage, Edward G. Ulmer* (London: Tantivy, 1974); Frederick Lamster, *Souls Made Great Through Love and Adversity: The Film Work of Frank Borzage* (Metuchen, NJ: Scarecrow, 1981).
13. Georges Sadoul, *Dictionary of Film Makers* (Berkeley, CA: University of California Press, 1972), 27.

14. Script is in Levien papers.
15. Quoted in "Bio," ibid.
16. Lamster, *Souls Made Great Through Love and Adversity*, 64.
17. Behrman, *Tribulations and Laughter*, 138, and "Bio." For Behrman's life and work, see Kenneth T. Reed, *S. N. Behrman* (Boston: Twayne, 1975).
18 S. N. Behrman, "You Can't Release Dante's 'Inferno' in the Summertime," *New York Times Magazine* (July 17, 1966), 30.
19. "The Brat" script, 37, Levien papers.
20. George Gershwin to Levien, August 21, 1931, ibid.
21. Edward Jablonski, *Gershwin* (New York: Doubleday, 1987), 299.
22. Levien to Joseph Verner Reed, February 7, 1933, Levien papers.
23. Behrman, *Tribulations and Laughter*, 178-82.
24. Sonya Levien, "Thirty Years Before the Mast," Levien papers. She had met him on one of her earlier London trips and *The Metropolitan* had published one of his stories (November 1921).
25. Levien, "Thirty Years Before the Mast."
26. *The Hollywood Reporter* (October 22, 1932, and February 3, 1933).
27. *The Warrior's Husband* script is in Levien papers.
28. James Wingate to Jason Joy, nd, ibid.
29. Levien file, Twentieth Century-Fox legal records.
30. Ibid.
31. Philip Dunne, *Take One: A Life in Movies and Politics* (New York: McGraw-Hill, 1980), 54.
32. Interview with Sheridan Gibney.
33. Mel Gussow, *Don't Say Yes Until I Finish Talking: A Biography of Darryl F. Zanuck* (Garden City, NY: Doubleday, 1971), 84-85.
34. Ibid., 70.
35. Unproduced script collection, UCLA Arts Library-Special Collections.
36. Diane Heckert, "Prize-Winning Movie Scripter," *Dayton Daily News* (November 30, 1954), D-1. In fact, Dafoe was anything but a simple country doctor. He would exploit the quints for huge sums of money and convince the Canadian government to remove them from their parents' custody to expedite his profiteering.
37. Background information is taken from publicity releases in *The Country Doctor* clipping file at the Herrick Library; conference notes from the Twentieth Century collection at the USC Cinema-Television Library; Johnson to Levien, October 1, 1935, Levien papers.
38. Twentieth Century-Fox publicity release, *The Country Doctor* clipping file, Herrick Library.
39. Levien to Dafoe, March 20, 1936, and Dafoe to Levien, March 25, 1936, Levien papers.
40. Conference notes, Twentieth Century-Fox collection, USC.
41. *Variety* (April 30, 1936), 6.

42. Zanuck to Levien, April 25, 1936, Levien papers.

43. *Variety* (May 8, 1936), 3; (July 29, 1937), 14; (June 29, 1938), 1. The best accounts of this event are in Larry Ceplair and Steven Englund, *The Inquisition in Hollywood: Politics in the Film Community, 1930-1960* (Garden City, N Y: Anchor Press/ Doubleday, 1980) and Nancy Lynn Schwartz, *The Hollywood Writers Wars* (New York: Knopf, 1982).

44. Quoted in Schwartz, *The Hollywood Writers Wars*, 73.

45. Twentieth Century-Fox legal records. Columbia and Universal raised strong protests against Twentieth's attempt at exclusive use of that title.

46. Los Angeles *Examine* (October 7, 1936).

47. Both treatments are in Levien papers. In January 1941, an Italian movie studio released the pro-Franco *Sin Novedad en Al Alcazar*. For an analysis of a Spanish Civil War movie written by a Communist, see Larry Ceplair, "The Politics of Compromise in Hollywood: A Case Study," *Cineaste* 8, no. 4 (nd), 2-7.

48. The sources for this discussion are the Kenneth Macgowan papers, Special Collections, University Research Library, UCLA, and the Twentieth Century-Fox collection at USC. Busch received an Academy Award nomination for best original story.

49. Macgowan papers and Twentieth Century-Fox collection.

50. "Falling Star," script, 32, Levien papers.

51. Four letters from Knopf to Levien, ibid., and Conn to Levien. No part of the manuscript is in the Levien papers.

52. Levien to Luhan, September 12, 1937, ibid.

53. Twentieth Century-Fox collection, USC; E. C. de Lavigne to George Wasson, January 17, 1938, Twentieth Century Fox legal records, UCLA.

54. Los Angeles *Examiner* (March 22, 1938).

55. Twentieth Century-Fox collection; Levien papers.

56. Garson Kanin, *Hollywood* (New York: Viking, 1967), 82-96; Robert Ardrey, "Roots..." *California Magazine* (August 1984), 93; *The American Film Institute Catalog: Feature Films, 1931-1940* (Berkeley, CA: University of California Press, 1993), 1:408-409; Carol Easton, *The Search for Sam Goldwyn* (New York: Morrow, 1976), 163; Arthur Marx, *Goldwyn: A Biography of the Man Behind the Myth* (New York: Norton, 1976), 254-55; *New York Times* (November 25, 1938), 19.

57. "The Cowboy and the Lady" script, 162-63, Herrick Library.

58. Edmonds to Carl Hovey, January 6, 1939, Levien papers.

59. Twentieth Century-Fox collection, USC; Zanuck to Levien, Levien papers.

60. Twentieth Century-Fox collection, USC. *Tin Pan Alley*, produced by Kenneth Macgowan and credited to Pamela Harris, Robert Ellis, and Helen Logan, was released by Fox in November 1940.

61. *Variety* (December 30, 1938), 1.

62. Levien to Wasson, June 10, 1939, Twentieth Century-Fox legal records.

63. "Man Hunt" correspondence and manuscript are in Levien papers.

64. F. Tennyson Jesse and H. M. Harwood, *London Front: Letters Written to America, 1939-1940* (New York: Doubleday, Doran, 1941), 83.

Chapter 6

1. Tamara Hovey, *Among the Survivors* (New York: Orion, 1971). She also wrote two biographies for children: *John Reed: Witness to Revolution* (1975) and *A Mind of Her Own: A Life of the Writer George Sand* (1977).

2. In early 1940, Levien worked at Walter Wanger Productions on a script about John C. and Jesse Benton Frémont. *So Gallantly Gleaming* was not produced.

3. Levien to Fryn Harwood, May 22, 1941, Levien papers.

4. Ibid., July 3, 1940. The theme of European children coming to the United States became the basis for a novelette she wrote that year, *The Man Who Lived Alone*. A reclusive young millionaire inventor and test pilot (Howard Hughes?) gets cajoled into adopting three children, one each from France, Belgium, and the Netherlands. A spunky young female newspaper reporter (Jean Arthur?) becomes involved. Following the usual convolutions and misunderstandings, they marry and adopt the children. Levien papers.

5. Levien to Harwood, May 22, 1941, ibid.

6. Ibid.

7. Ibid., October 1, 1941; Hovey to Perkins, January 29, 1942, Frances Perkins papers, part II-D, reel 9, Rare Books and Manuscripts Library, Columbia University.

8. Levien to Harwood, December 15, 1941, Levien papers.

9. Wallis to R. J. Obringer, March 17, 1941, *Rhapsody in Blue* Story File, Warner Bros. Archive, USC Cinema-Television Library.

10. *New York Times* (July 8, 1945).

11. Elsie Goldberg on behalf of her late husband, Isaac's, *George Gershwin* (New York: Simon & Schuster, 1931), received $2,500. B. M. Lytton-Edwards, for her radio play, *He Wrote the Rhapsody in Blue*, broadcast on BBC (June 1941), received £385. The correspondence regarding these claims is in the *Rhapsody in Blue* folder, Warner Bros. Archive.

12. Interview with Budd Schulberg; interview with William Fadiman.

13. Thomas Schatz, *The Genius of the System: Hollywood Filmmaking in the Studio Era* (New York: Pantheon, 1988), 359-60; Bosley Crowther, *The Lion's Roar. The Story of an Entertainment Empire* (New York: Dutton, 1957), 286-87; Hovey to Frances Perkins, December 23, 1944, Perkins papers.

14. Ibid.

Endnotes

15. *Look* (June 12, 1945), 76.
16. Hovey to Perkins, November 16, 1946, Perkins papers.
17. Script file, M-G-M Archive, USC Cinema-Television Library.
18. O'Hara to David Brown, February 6, 1957, in Matthew J. Bruccoli, ed., *Selected Letters of John O' Hara* (New York: Random House, 1978), 262; Frank MacShane, *The Life of John O'Hara* (New York: Dutton, 1980), 130-31; *Cass Timberlane* script file, M-G-M Archive.
19. *Quo Vadis* script file, M-G-M Archive; John Huston, *An Open Book* (New York: Knopf, 1980), 175-76; Lawrence Grabel, *The Hustons* (New York: Scribner's, 1989), 330-31; Mervyn LeRoy, *Mervyn LeRoy: Take One* (New York: Hawthorn, 1979), 169, 388-89, 393-94. Behrman did not comment on it in his memoir. (Without explanation, M-G-M dropped the question mark from the title—a Latin phrase meaning "whither goest thou?")
20. For Ludwig's own story, see Lee Server, *Screenwriter: Words Become Pictures* (Pittstown, NJ: Main Street, 1987).
21. Schary to Joe Pasternak, Levien to Schary, and preview results are in the Joe Pasternak collection, USC Cinema-Television Library. Speech is in Levien papers.
22. Levien to Luhan, November 21, 1950, Levien papers; interview with Joan Scott.
23. Laurel Award material is in Levien papers; Levien to Father James Keller, January 24, 1952, ibid. She also collected twelve Blue Ribbon Awards from *Box Office* magazine, given to the movie in general release which the National Screen Council deemed the most worthy for family viewing. (The next highest total was Helen Deutsch's, six.)
24. *Bhowani Junction* script file, M-G-M Archive; George Cukor papers, Margaret Herrick Library; Patrick McGilligan, *George Cukor: A Double Life* (New York: St. Martin's, 1991), 243. Emanuel Levy, who interviewed producer Pandro Berman, writes that Cukor disliked the Levien-Moffat script so much that he sent their draft to the book's author, John Masters, for a rewrite, without telling anyone. *George Cukor, Master of Elegance: Hollywood's Legendary Director and His Stars* (New York: Morrow, 1994), 233.
25. Levien to Harwood, May 10, 1955, Levien papers.
26. *The Hollywood Reporter* (October 11, 1956), 1.
27. Levien to Harwood, May 6, 1957, Levien papers.
28. "Thirty Years Before the Mast," ibid.
29. McGilligan claims that she wrote the first script for Cukor's *The Chapman Report* (*George Cukor*, 266), but the Warner Bros. material at USC indicates that Helen Deutsch wrote the first script, and there is no mention of Levien in the *Chapman* material in the Cukor papers.

Filmography

1919

Who Will Marry Me?
    Bluebird Photoplays; Paul Powell, dir.
    Story by Sonya Levien; scenario by Fred Myton
    Starring Carmel Myers and Thurston Hall

1921

Cheated Love
    Universal Film Manufacturing Co.; King Baggot, dir.
    Scenario by Lucien Hubbard, Sonya Levien, Doris Schroeder; additional story by Sonya Levien (Remake of *The Heart of a Jewess*. 1913)
    Starring Carmel Myers and George B. Williams

First Love
    Realart Pictures (Paramount Pictures); Maurice Campbell, dir.
    Story by Sonya Levien; scenario by Percy Heath and Aubrey Stauffer
    Starring Constance Binney and Warner Baxter

1922

The Top of New York
    Realart Pictures; Jesse Lasky, prod.; William D. Taylor, dir.
    Story by Sonya Levien; adaptation by George Hopkins
    Starring May McAvoy and Walter McGrail

Pink Gods
    Famous Players-Lasky (Paramount); Jesse Lasky, prod.; Penrhyn Stanlaws, dir.
    Based on Cynthia Stockley, "Pink Gods and Blue Demons"; adaptation by J. E. Nash and Sonya Levien; scenario by Ewart Adamson
    Starring Bebe Daniels and James Kirkwood

1923

The Snow Bride
    Famous Players-Lasky; Henry Kolker, dir.
    Story by Sonya Levien and Julie Herne; scenario by Sonya Levien
    Starring Alice Brady and Maurice B. Flynn

The Exciters
    Famous Players-Lasky; Maurice Campbell, dir.
    Based on the play by Martin Brown; scenario by John Colton and Sonya Levien
    Starring Bebe Daniels and Antonio Moreno

1925

Salome of the Tenements
    Famous Players-Lasky; Sidney Olcott, dir.
    Based on Anzia Yezierska, *Salome of the Tenements*; scenario by Sonya Levien
    Starring Jetta Goudal and Godfrey Tearle

1926

The Love Toy
    Warner Bros.; Erle C. Kenton, dir.
    Story by Charles Logue; scenario by Sonya Hovey
    Starring Lowell Sherman and Jane Winton

Why Girls Go Back Home
   Warner Bros.; James Flood, dir.
   Based on story by Catherine Brady; adaptation by Walter Morosco; scenario by Sonya Hovey
   Starring Patsy Ruth Miller and Clive Brook

Footloose Widows
   Warner Bros.; Roy Del Ruth, dir.
   Based on Beatrice Burton, *Footloose;* adaptation by Sonya Hovey and Sidney Toler; scenario by Darryl F. Zanuck
   Starring Louise Fazenda and Jacqueline Logan

Christine of the Big Tops
   Banner Productions (Sterling Pictures Distributing Corp.); Archie Mayo, dir.
   Story and scenario by Sonya Levien
   Starring Pauline Garon and Cullen Landis

1927

The Princess from Hoboken
   Tiffany Productions; Allan Dale, dir.
   Story and scenario by Sonya Levien
   Starring Edmund Burns and Blanche Mehaffey

The Heart Thief
   Metropolitan Pictures; John C. Flinn, prod.; Nils Olaf Cirsander, dir.
   Based on Lajos Biro, *The Highwayman*; adaptation by Gladys Unger; continuity by Sonya Levien; titles by Lesley Mason
   Starring Joseph Schildkraut and Lya De Putti

A Harp in Hock
   DeMille Pictures; Renaud Hoffman, dir.
   Based on story by Evelyn Campbell; continuity by Sonya Levien

Starring Rudolph Schildkraut, Junior Coghlan, May Robson, and Bessie Love

1928

A Ship Comes In
DeMille Pictures; William K. Howard, dir.
Story and adaptation by Julian Josephson; scenario by Sonya Levien; titles by John Krafft
Starring Rudolph Schildkraut and Louise Dresser

The Power of the Press
Columbia Pictures; Jack Cohn, prod.; Frank Capra, dir.
Story by Frederick A. Thompson; adaptation and continuity by Frederick A. Thompson and Sonya Levien
Starring Douglas Fairbanks, Jr. and Jobyna Ralston

1929

The Younger Generation
Columbia Pictures; Jack Cohn, prod.; Frank Capra, dir.
Based on Fannie Hurst, "Goldfish"; scenario by Sonya Levien; dialogue by Howard Green
Starring Jean Hersholt and Ricardo Cortez

Trial Marriage
Columbia Pictures; Erle C. Kenton, dir.
Story and scenario by Sonya Levien
Starring Norman Kerry and Sally Eilers

Behind That Curtain
Fox Film Corp.; Irving Cummings, dir.
Based on novel by Earl der Biggers; scenario by Sonya Levien and Clarke Silvernail
Starring Warner Baxter and Lois Moran

Lucky Star
   Fox Film Corp.; Frank Borzage, dir.
   Based on Tristan Tupper, "Three Episodes in the Life of Timothy Osborn"; scenario by Sonya Levien; dialogue by John Hunter Rooth
   Starring Charles Farrell and Janet Gaynor

They Had to See Paris
   Fox Film Corp.; Frank Borzage, dir.
   Based on novel by Homer Cray; scenario by Sonya Levien; dialogue by Owen Davis
   Starring Will Rogers and Irene Rich

Frozen Justice
   Fox Film Corp.; Allan Dwan, dir.
   Based on a novel by Ejnar Mikkelsen; scenario by Sonya Levien; dialogue by Owen Davis
   Starring Lenore Ulric and Robert Frazer

South Sea Rose
   Fox Film Corp.; Allan Dwan, dir.
   Based on Edward Sheldon and Tom Cushing's play, *La Gringa*; scenario by Sonya Levien; dialogue by Elliott Lester
   Starring Lenore Ulric and Charles Bickford

1930

Song O' My Heart
   Fox Film Corp.; Frank Borzage, dir.
   Based on a story by J. J. McCarthy; adaptation by Tom Barry; continuity by Sonya Levien
   Starring John McCormack, Alice Joyce, and Maureen O'Sullivan

So This is London
   Fox Film Corp.; John Blystone, dir.

Based on the play by Arthur Goodrich; adaptation and dialogue by Owen Davis; scenario by Sonya Levien
Starring Will Rogers and Irene Rich

Liliom
Fox Film Corp.; Frank Borzage, dir.
Based on Ferenc Molnar play; continuity by Sonya Levien; screenplay and dialogue by S. N. Behrman
Starring Charles Farrell and Rose Hobart

Lightnin'
Fox Film Corp.; Henry King, dir.
Based on play by Winchell Smith and Frank Bacon; adaptation and dialogue by S. N. Behrman and Sonya Levien (remake of 1925 movie)
Starring Will Rogers and Louise Dresser

1931

Daddy Long Legs
Fox Film Corp.; Alfred Santell, dir.
Based on the play by Jean Webster; screenplay and dialogue by Sonya Levien; additional dialogue by S. N. Behrman (remake of 1919 movie)
Starring Janet Gaynor and Warner Baxter

The Brat
Fox Film Corp.; John Ford, dir.
Based on the play by Maude Fulton; screenplay by S. N. Behrman and Sonya Levien
Starring Sally O'Neill and Alan Dinehart

Surrender
Fox Film Corp.; William K. Howard, dir.
Based on Pierre Benoit's play *Axelle*; screenplay by S. N. Behrman and Sonya Levien
Starring Warner Baxter and Leila Hyams

Delicious
   Fox Film Corp.; David Butler, dir.
   Story by Guy Bolton; screenplay by Sonya Levien and Guy Bolton
   Starring Janet Gaynor and Charles Farrell

1932

She Wanted a Millionaire
   Fox Film Corp.; John G. Blystone, dir.
   Story and continuity by Sonya Levien; adaptation and dialogue by William Anthony McGuire
   Starring Joan Bennett and Spencer Tracy

After Tomorrow
   Fox Film Corp.; Frank Borzage, dir.
   Based on the play by John Golden and Hugh Strange; adaptation and dialogue by Sonya Levien
   Starring Charles Farrell and Marion Nixon

Rebecca of Sunnybrook Farm
   Fox Film Corp.; Alfred Santell, dir.
   Based on the novel by Kate Douglass Wiggin and Charlotte Thompson; adaptation and dialogue by S. N. Behrman and Sonya Levien (remake of 1921 movie)
   Starring Marion Nixon and Ralph Bellamy

Tess of the Storm Country
   Fox Film Corp.; Alfred Santell, dir.
   Based on the novel by Grace Miller White; screenplay by Sonya Levien and S. N. Behrman (remake of 1914 and 1922 movies)
   Starring Janet Gaynor and Charles Farrell

1933

Cavalcade
 Fox Film Corp.; Winfield Sheehan, prod.; Frank Lloyd, dir.
 Based on the play by Noël Coward; screenplay by Reginald Berkeley; continuity edited by Sonya Levien
 Starring Clive Brook and Diane Wynyard

State Fair
 Fox Film Corp.; Winfield Sheehan, prod.; Henry King, dir.
 Based on the novel by Phil Stong; screenplay by Paul Green and Sonya Levien (remade in 1945 and 1962)
 Starring Will Rogers and Janet Gaynor

The Warrior's Husband
 Fox Film Corp.; Jesse Lasky, prod.; Walter Lang, dir.
 Based on the play by Julian Thompson; adaptation and dialogue by Ralph Spence; continuity by Sonya Levien
 Starring Elissa Landi and Marjorie Rambeau

Berkeley Square
 Fox Film Corp.; Jesse Lasky, prod.; Frank Lloyd, dir.
 Based on the play by John L. Balderston; screenplay by Sonya Levien and John L. Balderston
 Starring Leslie Howard and Heather Angel

Mr. Skitch
 Fox Film Corp.; James Cruze, dir.
 Based on Anne Cameron, *Green Dice;* screenplay by Ralph Spence and Sonya Levien
 Starring Will Rogers and ZaSu Pitts

1934

As Husbands Go
 Fox Film Corp.; Jesse Lasky, prod.; Hamilton McFadden, dir.

Based on the play by Rachel Crothers; screenplay by Sonya Levien; additional dialogue by S. N. Behrman
Starring Warner Baxter and Helen Vinson

Change of Heart
Fox Film Corp.; John G. Blystone, dir.
Based on Kathleen Norris, *Manhattan Love Song*; screenplay by Sonya Levien and James Gleason; additional dialogue by Samuel Hoffenstein
Starring Janet Gaynor and Charles Farrell

The White Parade
Fox Film Corp.; Jesse Lasky, prod.; Irving Cummings, dir.
Based on the novel by Rian James; screenplay by Sonya Levien and Ernest Pascal
Starring Loretta Young and John Boles

1935

Here's To Romance
Twentieth Century-Fox; Jesse Lasky, prod.; Alfred E. Green, dir.
Story by Sonya Levien and Ernest Pascal; screenplay by Ernest Pascal and Arthur Richman
Starring Nino Martini and Genevieve Tobin

Navy Wife
Twentieth Century-Fox; Allan Dwan, dir.
Based on Kathleen Norris, *Beauty's Daughter*; screenplay by Sonya Levien; additional dialogue by Edmund T. Lowe
Starring Claire Trevor and Ralph Bellamy

1936

The Country Doctor
Twentieth Century-Fox; Henry King, dir.
Story idea by Charles E. Blake; screenplay by Sonya Levien
Starring Jean Hersholt and June Lang

Reunion
>Twentieth Century-Fox; Norman Taurog, dir.
>Story by Bruce Gould; screenplay by Sonya Levien, Sam Hellman, and Gladys Lehman
>Starring Jean Hersholt and Rachelle Hudson

1938

In Old Chicago
>Twentieth Century-Fox; Kenneth Macgowan, prod.; Henry King, dir.
>Story by Niven Busch; screenplay by Sonya Levien and Lamar Trotti
>Starring Tyrone Power, Alice Fay, and Don Ameche

Kidnapped
>Twentieth Century-Fox; Kenneth Macgowan, prod.; Alfred L. Werker, dir.
>Based on the novel by Robert Louis Stevenson; screenplay by Sonya Levien, Eleanor Harris, Ernest Pascal, and Edwin Blum
>Starring Warner Baxter and Freddie Bartholomew

Four Men and a Prayer
>Twentieth Century-Fox; Kenneth Macgowan, prod.; John Ford, dir.
>Based on the novel by David Garth; screenplay by Sonya Levien, Richard Sherman, and Walter Ferris
>Starring Loretta Young, Richard Greene, George Sanders, and David Niven

The Cowboy and the Lady
>Samuel Goldwyn Pictures; H. C. Potter, dir.
>Story idea by Leo McCarey and Frank R. Adams; screenplay by Sonya Levien and S. N. Behrman
>Starring Gary Cooper and Merle Oberon

1939

Drums Along the Mohawk
   Twentieth Century-Fox; Raymond Griffith, prod.; John Ford, dir.
   Based on the novel by Walter Edmonds; screenplay by Sonya Levien and Lamar Trotti
   Starring Claudette Colbert and Henry Fonda

The Hunchback of Notre Dame
   RKO Pictures; Pandro S. Berman, prod.; William Dieterle, dir.
   Based on Victor Hugo, *Notre Dame de Paris*; adaptation by Bruno Frank; screenplay by Sonya Levien
   Starring Charles Laughton, Cedric Hardwicke, and Maureen O'Hara

1941

Ziegfeld Girl
   M-G-M; Pandro S. Berman, prod.; Robert Z. Leonard, dir.
   Screenplay by Sonya Levien and Marguerite Roberts
   Starring James Stewart, Judy Garland, *inter alia*

1943

The Amazing Mrs. Holliday
   Universal Pictures; Bruce Manning, dir.
   Story by Sonya Levien; adaptation by Boris Ingster and Leo Townsend; screenplay by John Jacoby and Frank Ryan
   Starring Deanna Durbin

1945

Rhapsody in Blue
   Warner Bros.; Jesse L. Lasky, prod.; Irving Rapper, dir.

Story by Sonya Levien; screenplay by Howard Koch and Elliot Paul
Starring Robert Alda and Joan Leslie

The Valley of Decision
M-G-M; Edwin H. Knopf, prod.; Tay Garnett, dir.
Based on the novel by Marcia Davenport; screenplay by John Meehan and Sonya Levien
Starring Greer Garson and Gregory Peck

1946

The Green Years
M-G-M; Leon Gordon, prod,; Victor Saville, dir.
Based on the novel by A. J. Cronin; screenplay by Robert Ardrey and Sonya Levien
Starring Charles Coburn, Dean Stockwell, Tom Drake, Hume Cronin, and Jessica Tandy

1947

Cass Timberlane
M-G-M; Arthur Hornblow, Jr., prod.; George Sidney, dir.
Based on the novel by Sinclair Lewis; adaptation by Sonya Levien and Donald Ogden Stewart; screenplay by Donald Ogden Stewart
Starring Spencer Tracy and Lana Turner

1948

Three Daring Daughters
M-G-M; Joe Pasternak, prod.; Fred M. Wilcox, dir.
Screenplay by Albert Mannheimer, Frederick Kohner, Sonya Levien, and John Meehan
Starring Jeanette MacDonald, Jose Iturbi, and Jane Powell

1951

The Great Caruso
M-G-M; Joe Pasternak, prod.; Richard Thorpe, dir.
Suggested by Dorothy Caruso's biography; screenplay by Sonya Levien and William Ludwig
Starring Mario Lanza and Ann Blyth

Quo Vadis
M-G-M; Sam Zimbalist, prod.; Mervin LeRoy, dir.
Based on the novel by Henryk Synkiewicz; screenplay by John Lee Mahin, S. N. Behrman, and Sonya Levien
Starring Robert Taylor, Deborah Kerr, and Peter Ustinov

1952

The Merry Widow
M-G-M; Joe Pasternak, prod.; Curtis Bernhardt, dir.
Based on the operetta by Franz Lehar; screenplay by Sonya Levien and William Ludwig (remake of 1925 and 1934 movies)
Starring Fernando Lamas and Lana Turner

1954

The Student Prince
M-G-M; Joe Pasternak, prod.; Richard Thorpe, dir.
Based on Wilhelm Meyer-Foerster's play *Old Heidelberg* and the operetta by Dorothy Donnelly and Sigmund Romberg; screenplay by William Ludwig and Sonya Levien (remake of 1927 movie)
Starring Edmumd Purdom and Ann Blyth

1955

Hit the Deck
 M-G-M; Joe Pasternak, prod.; Roy Rowland, dir.
 Based on Hubert Osborn, *Shore Leave* and the play by Herbert Fields; screenplay by Sonya Levien and William Ludwig
 Starring Tony Martin and Jane Powell

Interrupted Melody
 M-G-M; Jack Cummings, prod.; Curtis Bernhardt, dir.
 Screenplay by William Ludwig and Sonya Levien
 Starring Eleanor Parker and Glenn Ford

Oklahoma!
 Magna Theatre Corp.; Arthur Hornblow, Jr., prod.; Fred Zinnemann, dir.
 Based on Lynn Riggs' play *Green Grow the Lilacs* and Richard Rodgers and Oscar Hammerstein's *Oklahoma!*; screenplay by Sonya Levien and William Ludwig
 Starring Gordon Macrae and Shirley Jones

1956

Bhowani Junction
 M-G-M; Pandro S. Berman, prod.; George Cukor, dir.
 Based on the novel by John Masters; screenplay by Sonya Levien and Ivan Moffit
 Starring Ava Gardner and Stewart Granger

1957

Jeanne Eagels
 Columbia Pictures; George Sidney, prod. and dir.
 Screenplay by Daniel Fuchs, Sonya Levien, and John Fante
 Starring Kim Novak and Jeff Chandler

1960

Pepe
 Columbia Pictures; George Sidney, prod. and dir.
 Story by Sonya Levien and Leonard Spigelgass; screenplay by Dorothy Kingsley and Claude Binyon
 Starring Cantinflas

Uncredited Script Work

1928
 Let 'er Go Gallegher, DeMille Pictures, adaptation

1929
 The Quitter, Columbia Pictures, screenplay

1931
 Bad Girl, Fox Film Corp., continuity and dialogue
 Annabelle's Affairs, Fox, continuity and dialogue
 The Man Who Came Back, Fox, rewrites

1932
 Society Girl, Fox, rewrites

1934
 Marie Galante, Fox, screenplay
 David Harum, Fox, rewrites

1935
 Curly Top, Fox, rewrites
 Music is Magic, Fox, rewrite
 Gentle Julia, Fox, rewrites

1939
 Ramona, Columbia Pictures, rewrites
 Belle Starr, Twentieth Century-Fox, treatment
 Maryland, Twentieth Century-Fox, original story

1945
The Enchanted Cottage, RKO Pictures, treatment

1947
Desire Me, M-G-M, co-screenplay

Unproduced Screenplays

1925
A Girl of the Circus: romance melodrama with gags; orphaned girl meets playboy inventor.

1929
Playmates, Fox Film Corp.: costume romance, set in Budapest, intended for Janet Gaynor, co-written with Elliott Lester.

1930
The Country Doctor, Fox Film Corp.: western rural doctor as self-sacrificing healer and sage, co-written with Don Marquis and Izola Forrester

1934
The Captive Bride, Fox Film Corp.: Representative of Mussolini's government comes to United States to sign oil deal and falls in love with oilman's daughter. Based on *The Proud Princess* by Edward Sheldon and Dorothy Donnelly.

1936
The Siege of the Alcazar, Twentieth Century-Fox: Original story about the Spanish Civil War, focusing on the Franco side.

1937
Falling Star, Twentieth: Satire on Hollywood, co-written with Richard Sherman.
Merry, Merry Maidens, Selznick International

1938
The Postman Walks Alone, Twentieth: A do-good postman

founds American Legion baseball, intended for Don Ameche.

Uncensored, Twentieth: Account of anti-German underground activity in Belgium during World War I. Based on Oscar E. Millard, *Libre Belgique*.

1939

So Gallantly Gleaming, Walter Wanger Productions: Biography of Jesse Benton and John C. Frémont.

1942

The Rumelharts of Rampler Avenue (*Hello Neighbor*): Hillbillies squat in wealthy neighborhood, co-written with Paul Green.

1953

The Gay Girls, Columbia Pictures: Musical comedy of the "My Sister, Eileen" variety, co-written with William Ludwig

1955

Joseph and His Brethren, Columbia: Revised treatment of a screenplay by Clifford Odets, co-written with Mann Rubin.

1956

Raquel: The Jewess of Toledo, M-G-M: Based on the novel by Lion Feuchtwanger.

1959

The Running of the Tide, M-G-M: Salem, Mass. sea story melodrama, set in 1800, co-written with Robert Thomsen.

The Sword and the Cross, Samuel Bronston Productions: Life of Jesus, co-written with John Farrow.

Undated

Why Girls Go Back Home [1926-27?]: Melodrama with comedy-farce interludes.

Wild Man's Luck (Paramount, [1926?]): Canadian fur trapper returns to Northland sweetheart after bitter experience with Broadway gold digger.

Index

Academy of Motion Picture Arts and Sciences, 83
Acker, Ally, 42
Akins, Zoë, 21, 49, 72, 111
The Amazing Mrs. Holliday, 106
Ameche, Don, 84-85
Among the Survivors, 64, 103-105
Anarchism, 4, 7, 8, 67-68
Antin, Mary, 59
Ardrey, Robert, 96, 116
Arlen, Harold, 79
Authors' League of America, 70, 88

Baird, Leah, 42
Banner Productions, 67
Barrie, James M., 34
Barzman, Ben, 48
Behind that Curtain, 75
Behrman, S. N., 16, 63, 72-73, 76-80, 96, 113
Belle Starr, 98
Beranger, Clara, 46
Bergson, Henri, 28
Berkeley, Reginald, 80
Berlin, Irving, 98
Berman, Pandro, 105
Bernstein, Aline, 51
Berry, John, 115
Bhowani Junction, 116-17
Biggers, Earl Der, 75
The Big Parade, 38
Biograph Company, 44

The Birth of a Nation, 55
Blackwell, Alice Stone, 15
Blake, Charles E., 86-87
Bloch, Stella, 49
Bluebird Photoplays, 53
Blum, Edwin, 92-93
Bolsheviks, 8, 27
Bolton, Guy, 75, 78
Borzage, Frank, 72, 75-77, 80
Bosworth, Inc., 45
Bourke-White, Margaret, 51
Brady, William, 45
The Brat, 78
Breen, Richard, 116
Brennan, Walter, 98
Bronston, Samuel, 120
Brownlow, Kevin, 59
Bryan, William Jennings, 19
Bryant, Louise, 28
Buck, Pearl, 97
Busch, Niven, 91, 98

Cahan, Abraham, 2, 5
Calhoun, Dorothy, 46
Campbell, Alan, 96
Capra, Frank, 69, 97
The Captive Bride, 85
Careers for Women, 73
Caruso, Enrico, 113
Cass Timberlane, 109, 111-12
Cavalcade, 80-82
Chan, Charlie, 75
Chandlee, Harry, 108

Change of Heart, 81
Cheated Love, 53
Christine of the Big Top, 67
Coffee, Lenore, 43, 45-46, 70
Cohn, Harry, 118
Cole, Lester, 40, 110-11
Collier, John, 67
Collins, Richard, 91
Columbia Pictures, 69, 83, 107-108, 114, 118-19
Conference of Studio Unions, 110
Conrad, Joseph, 21
Cooper, Gary, 95-96
Copeland, Charles Townsend, 16
The Country Doctor, 85-87
Coward, Noël, 80-81
The Cowboy and the Lady, 95-97
Crawford, William, 73
Cukor, George, 48-49, 116-17
Cunard, Grace, 46
Curly Top, 72

Daddy Long Legs, 72, 78
Dafoe, Dr. Allan Roy, 86-87
Davenport, Marcia, 109-10
Day, Clarence, Jr., 21, 29-31, 63, 67
Delicious, 75, 78-79
DeMille, Cecil B., 33, 42, 46, 63, 67
de Mille, William C., 38, 46
Dewey, John, 56, 59
Dionne quintuplets, 85-88
Dix, Beulah Marie, 46
Dorr, Rheta Childe, 21
"Doubling in Love," 66
Dramatists Guild, 88
Dreiser, Theodore, 21
Drums Along the Mohawk, 97-98
Dunne, Philip, 84
Durbin, Deanna, 106
Dwan, Allan, 72

Eastman, Crystal, 21, 27
The Eddy Duchin Story, 119
Edmunds, Walter D., 97

Educational Alliance, 9-10
Ellis, Havelock, 22
Emerson, John, 42, 96
Eminent Authors Pictures, Inc., 36, 37, 46
The Enchanted Cottage, 99
The Exciters, 55

Fadiman, William, 108
Fairfax, Marion, 46
The Falling Star, 93
Famous Players-Lasky Film Corp., 31, 53-56, 59
Farrell, Charles, 72, 75-77, 79, 81
Fascism, 85, 89-91
Faulkner, William, 97
Faye, Alice, 84
Ferber, Edna, 21
Feuchtwanger, Lion, 118
First Love, 54
Fitzgerald, F. Scott, 39
Five of a Kind, 88
Footloose Widows, 67, 85
Ford, John, 72, 78
Four Men and a Prayer, 94
Fox, William, 45, 59, 71, 79
Fox Film Corp., 46, 63, 68, 70-84
Franco, Francisco, 89-91
Frank, Leonhard, 110
Frankfurter, Felix, 28
Friedman, Philip Alan, 14

Galsworthy, John, 21
Garson, Greer, 110
Garson, Harry, 45-46
Gauntier, Gene, 46
Gaynor, Janet, 72, 75-76, 78-79, 81, 84
Gershwin, George, 78-79, 107
Gershwin, Ira, 78-79, 107
Gibney, Sheridan, 84
Gilman, Charlotte Perkins, 21
Glass, Montague, 57-58
Glyn, Elinor, 72

Index

Gold, Lee, 115
Gold, Tamara Hovey, 56, 64, 103, 106, 115
Goldwyn, Samuel, 36, 56, 59, 95-96
Goldwyn, Samuel, Jr., 47
Goldwyn Pictures Corp., 47, 63, 70
The Good Earth, 97
Gray, Hugh, 113
The Great Caruso, 109, 113-14
Green, Paul, 81
The Green Years, 109
Griffith, D. W., 44

Hackett, Walter, 90
Hampton, Benjamin, 36-38
Hapgood, Hutchins, 16
A Harp in Hock, 67
Harris, Eleanor, 92-93
Harwood, Fryn (*see also* F. Tennyson Jesse), 105-106, 118
Hays, Will H., 35
Heart of a Jewess, 53
The Heart Thief, 67
Hellman, Lillian, 96
Hellman, Sam, 87
Henie, Sonja, 84, 95
Herron, George D., 20
Hersholt, Jean, 87
Heterodoxy, 21
Hillquit, Morris, 20
Hit the Deck, 116
Hoffenstein, Samuel, 119
Hopper, E. Mason, 58
Hornblow, Arthur, Jr., 112-13
House Committee on Un-American Activities, 115
Howe, Frederic C., 22
Howe, Marie Jenny, 21
Hovey, Carl, 16-17, 19, 26, 28-29, 38, 63-64, 66, 101, 105-10, 115, 118
Hovey, Serge, 54-55, 106, 115
Hughes, Rupert, 37-38
Hugo, Victor, 99

Hume, Cyril, 113
The Hunchback of Notre Dame, 99, 105
Hungry Hearts, 56-59
Hurst, Fannie, 69
Huston, John, 113

Ince, Thomas H., 37, 46
Industrial Workers of the World, 7-8, 20
In Old Chicago, 91-92
International Alliance of Theatrical Stage Employees, 110
Interrupted Melody, 115-16
Irwin, Inez Haynes, 21, 27

Jacobs, Lewis, 33
James, William, 28
Jeanne Eagels, 119
Jesse, F. Tennyson (*see also* Fryn Harwood), 100
Jewish culture, 1-8, 61-62
Johnson, Nunnally, 86
Joseph and His Brethren, 120
Josephson, Julian, 57-58, 81

Kanin, Garson, 96
Keller, Helen, 20
Kentucky, 98
Kenyon, Curtis, 92
Kidnapped, 92-93
King, Henry, 81
Kingsley, Sidney, 112
Kipling, Rudyard, 21-22
Knickerbocker, H. R., 90
Knopf, Blanche, 93
Koch, Howard, 108
Kropotkin, Peter, 4, 7
Kummer, Claire, 72

Lang, Jennings, 116
Laski, Harold, 28
Lasky, Jesse, 28, 35, 81-82, 108
Lawrence, Marjorie, 116

Lehman, Gladys, 87
Lehr, Abraham, 58, 63
Leopold and Loeb case, 61-62
LeRoy, Mervyn, 113
Levant, Oscar, 79, 108
Lewis, Sinclair, 14, 111-12
Lightnin', 78
Liliom, 76-77
Loew's, Inc., 71, 83
Loos, Anita, 41-42, 44, 47, 49, 96, 109
Lowrey, Carolyn, 42
Lucky Star, 75
Ludwig, William, 14, 28-29, 47, 63, 78, 89, 113-16
Luhan, Mabel Dodge, 19, 51, 93, 115

McCarey, Leo, 95-96
McCormack, John, 72, 76
Macgowan, Kenneth, 37, 39, 90-92
McGuinness, James K., 41
Macpherson, Jeanie, 33, 42, 46
Mahin, John Lee, 41
Male and Female, 34
Marion, Frances, 43, 45-47, 49, 75
Marx, Harpo, 79
Maryland, 98
Mast, Gerald, 41
Masters, John, 116
Mathis, June, 42, 46
Mayer, Louis B., 45-46, 113, 120
Meehan, John, 109, 112
Meredyth, Bess, 97
Merry, Merry Maidens, 94
The Merry Widow, 109, 115-16
Merwin, Samuel, 12
Metro Pictures Corp., 37, 42, 46
Metropolitan Pictures, 67
M-G-M (Metro-Goldwyn-Mayer, Inc.) 35, 39, 46, 70, 85, 88-89, 101, 105-18
Millard, Oscar E., 94
Mix, Tom, 106-107

Moffat, Ivan, 117
Molnar, Ferenc, 77
Motion Picture Producers and Distributors of America, 35, 83
Munro, H. H. (Saki), 21
Murfin, Jane, 46, 49

National American Woman Suffrage Association, 15
National Labor Relations Board, 88
Nazism, 100-101
Newspaper Guild, 88
The New York Hat, 44
New York University Law School, 11

Odets, Clifford, 107-108, 120
Office of War Information, 63, 101, 106-107, 109
O'Hara, John, 111-12
Oklahoma!, 114, 116
O'Neill, Eugene, 27
On the Town, 114
Opesken, Julius (Sonya's father), 1, 4-8, 28
Orient Express, 63
Orth, Marian, 72

Pacifist movements, 24
Pal Joey, 119
Paramount Pictures Corp., 35, 45, 47, 54, 71-72, 83, 85, 95
Parker, Dorothy, 47, 96
Parsons, Louella O., 90, 95
Pascal, Ernest, 92-93
Pathé, 67
Paul, Elliot, 108
Pearson, Virginia, 42
Peck, Gregory, 113
People's Institute, 22
Pepe, 119
Perkins, Frances, 14, 51, 89, 107, 110

Index

Pickford, Mary, 45
Pinero, Arthur Wing, 99
Pink Gods, 55
Poor Little Rich Girl, 45
Potter, H. C., 96
Power, Tyrone, 85
The Power of the Press, 69
The Princess from Hoboken, 67

The Quitter, 69
Quo Vadis, 109, 112-13

Radio Writers Guild, 88
Raquel: The Jewess of Toledo, 118
Reed, John, 20, 25-27, 109
Reisch, Walter, 113
Reunion, 87
Rhapsody in Blue, 79, 107-108
Richards, Sylvia, 115
Riskin, Robert, 96-97
RKO Radio Pictures, Inc., 47, 83, 99, 105
Roberts, Marguerite, 105, 111
Robinson, Casey, 110-11
Rodman, Henrietta, 21
Rogers, Will, 72-73, 76, 78, 81, 84, 86, 97
Roosevelt, Eleanor, 89
Roosevelt, Franklin D., 83, 89
Roosevelt, Theodore, 20, 25-27
Rossen, Robert, 107
Rosten, Leo, 40
Rubinstein, Helena, 51
Russia, 1-7
Ryan, Frank, 96

Sacco and Vanzetti case, 67
Sadoul, Georges, 75
St. John, Adela Rogers, 49
Salome of the Tenements, 56, 59-64
Sanger, Margaret, 27-28
Scala, Kathryn, 107
Schary, Dore, 113-14
Schenck, Joseph, 84

Schönberg, Arnold, 62, 79
Schulberg, Adeline, 5
Schulberg, Ben, 5
Schulberg, Budd, 5, 108
Scott, Joan, 115
Screen Playwrights, Inc., 88-89
Screen Writers Guild (Writers Guild of America West), 83-84, 88-89, 112, 114, 116
Selznick, Myron, 69
Selznick International Pictures, 94
Shall We Dance, 79
Shaw, George Bernard, 22
Sheehan, Winfield, 71-72, 75-77, 79-81, 84
A Ship Comes In, 67
Shipman, Nell, 42, 44
Sidney, George, 118
The Siege of the Alcazar, 90-91
Sinclair, May, 22
Slide, Anthony, 42
The Snow Bride, 55
Socialism, 11, 20, 25, 56
Song O' My Heart, 72, 76
So This is London, 72
Spanish Civil War, 89-91
State Fair, 81-82
Steffens, Lincoln, 16, 25
Stevens, George, 117
Stevenson, Robert Louis, 92-93
Stewart, Donald Ogden, 40, 112
Stokes, Rose Pastor, 10, 21, 27, 56, 59
Stokowski, Leopold, 79
Stong, Phil, 81
The Student Prince, 116
Sullivan, Gardner C., 37
Swanson, Gloria, 34
Swerling, Jo, 41
Synkiewicz, Henryk, 112

Taffel, Bess, 47-48
Taft, William Howard, 20
Tarkington, Booth, 21

Index

Temple, Shirley, 72, 84
Tess of the Storm Country, 79
Thalberg, Irving, 35, 70, 88-89, 112
They Had to See Paris, 72, 76
Three Daring Daughters, 109, 112
Three on a Honeymoon, 63
Tiffany Productions, 67
Top of New York, 31, 54
Trial Marriage, 69
Trotti, Lamar, 91-92, 97-98
Twentieth Century-Fox Film Corp., 39, 47, 84-99, 105

Uncensored, 94-95
Under the Crescent, 44
Underwood, Oscar, 20
Universal Pictures Corp. 35, 53, 106
University Settlement, 10-11

The Valley of Decision, 109-10
Van Upp, Virginia, 41
Veiller, Bernard, 37-38
Viertel, Salka, 49
Vorse, Mary Heaton, 21

Wallis, Hal, 107
Walsh, Raoul, 78

Warner Bros., 67, 79, 85, 94, 107-108
The Warrior's Husband, 82-83
Wasson, George, 99
Weber, Lois, 42, 45
Whigham, H. J., 19, 25
Whitney, Harry Payne, 19
Who Will Mary Me?, 53
Who Wrote the Movie . . . ?, 43
Wilson, Woodrow, 19, 25-26
Wodehouse, P. G., 21
A Woman of My Own, 111
Woman suffrage, 22-23
The Woman's Journal, 15-16
World Film Co., 45
Writers Club, 66, 70
Wurtzel, Sol, 77, 80
Wyler, William, 96

Yezierska, Anzia, 21, 56-61
Young, Clara Kimball, 45
The Younger Generation, 69

Zangwill, Israel, 22
Zanuck, Darryl F., 72, 84-94, 97-98
Ziegfeld Girl, 105-106
Zimbalist, Sam, 113
Zukor, Adolph, 36

About the Author

Larry Ceplair received his bachelor's degree from the University of California, Los Angeles, and his master's and doctorate from the University of Wisconsin. Currently, he teaches history at Santa Monica College. He is the co-author of *The Inquisition in Hollywood* (Anchor Doubleday, 1980), *The Public Years of Sarah and Angelina Grimké* (Columbia University Press, 1989) and *Charlotte Perkins Gilman: A Nonfiction Reader* (Columbia University Press, 1991).

OHIO UNIVERSITY LIBRARY
Please return this book as soon as you have finished with it. In order to avoid a fine it must be returned by the latest date stamped below. All books are subject to recall after two weeks or immediately if needed for reserve.

DEC 0 9 1997

NOV 2 5 1997
RETURN BY
OCT 1 4 1999

OCT 1 4 1999

NOV 1 9 1996